Orbis Sensualium Pictus

JOANNES AMOS COMENIUS

Orbis Sensualium Pictus

FACSIMILE OF THE THIRD LONDON EDITION 1672

With an Introduction by
JAMES BOWEN

SYDNEY UNIVERSITY PRESS
1967

SYDNEY UNIVERSITY PRESS
Press Building University of Sydney, N.S.W., Australia

U.S.A.: PENNSYLVANIA STATE UNIVERSITY PRESS

NEW ZEALAND: PRICE MILBURN AND COMPANY LIMITED

Elsewhere: METHUEN AND COMPANY LIMITED,
LONDON AND THEIR AGENTS

First published 1967

National Library of Australia registry number Aus 67-673

This book is published with support from the
Eleanor Sophia Wood Bequest

PRINTED AT THE GRIFFIN PRESS
ADELAIDE
and registered in Australia
for transmission by post as a book

CONTENTS

LIST OF PLATES

PREFACE

DESPITE the very large number of editions of *Orbis Sensualium Pictus* produced between 1658 and 1845, when it enjoyed wide use as a school book, few original copies survive. Those that do are treasured volumes preserved in collections of rare books. The last English-language reprinting was made in 1887 by the American publisher C. W. Bardeen whose version combined the illustrations from the first German edition with the London text of 1728, slightly modified and re-set in a nineteenth-century typeface. Even that edition has almost disappeared.

The present edition, the first in English this century, is a photolithographic facsimile of the third London edition of 1672, reproduced on a larger page. The choice of that particular edition has been determined by a number of factors, the most important being the quality of the photographic plates that could be obtained. In every respect the 1672 edition is almost identical with the original publication of Comenius as it appeared in the first English translation. This facsimile therefore is virtually a primary source.

Research funds for the study of all available volumes of *Orbis Sensualium Pictus* came initially from the University of Alberta in Canada and later from the University of New England in Australia. A number of libraries co-operated most willingly. In particular it is a pleasure to acknowledge the enthusiastic response of the Bodleian Library to the request for permission to use their excellent copy, from which photographic negatives were made by the Clarendon Press. The libraries of the University of Illinois and Cornell University kindly provided the plates to illustrate the later development of the book.

Most especially, I want to thank my wife who worked on the project since its inception and whose valuable contributions are evident to me in so many places.

JAMES BOWEN

University of New England
Armidale, Australia

INTRODUCTION

IN the year 1658 *Orbis Sensualium Pictus* was first published at Nuremberg in a Latin-German edition. Intended by its author to be an introductory text for teaching Latin quickly, pleasantly and effectively in the grammar school, it was unique in its day both in conception and appearance. Many of its features, such as the numerous illustrations, the encyclopedic organization of content and the use of the vernacular language alongside Latin, were radical innovations that departed markedly from the traditional form in which Latin grammars were presented.

The success of *Orbis Pictus,* the contracted title by which the book came to be known, was instantaneous. A Latin-English version was produced in London within a year of its original publication in Germany, and during the ensuing decade it appeared in at least ten editions, in the French, Italian and Polish vernaculars as well as German and English. In the remaining years of the seventeenth century, through all of the eighteenth and into the first decades of the nineteenth century, its popularity continued. Translations were made into many of the major languages of Europe and also into Arabic, Turkish, Persian and Mongolian. From its employment as one of the most popular school books in existence, its use spread into the home where it became a fascinating and diverting picture-book. Then, after almost two centuries of popularity, it disappeared rapidly from use.

Considering the difficult circumstances in which it was created and the obvious inconsistencies of its content, it is a tribute to the imaginative conception of the book that such a long time passed before it was superseded. The early popularity of *Orbis Pictus* did not lie in any exceptional aesthetic qualities; its physical format was comparatively crude. As early as the fifteenth century the crafts of typography and block printing had reached standards of technical and visual excellence superior to Comenius' publication. Its appeal stemmed in large part from the fact that, despite remarkable progress in the art of printing during the sixteenth and seventeenth centuries and the correlative growth of an erudite and cultured middle class in Europe, little attention had been given to the application of printing to school use.

Orbis Pictus was the first significant book designed to enlist the several possibilities of printing towards improving and facilitating learning. It combined line illustrations with a variety of typefaces—black-letter, roman, italic—to present effectively a content selected especially for children. Yet, despite its seemingly artless appearance and its modest attempt to exploit the potentialities of the graphic arts, *Orbis Pictus* had, at least for its author, Joannes Amos Comenius, a much deeper significance. It was part of his grand scheme to regenerate civilization itself.

Simple antiquarian charm is a recommendation to a study of *Orbis Pictus*; a full appreciation can proceed only from an understanding of the intellectual and educational purposes that it was designed to implement. The book appeared at the end of its author's career, and followed a lifetime of writing and publication. Although it was intended as the first and simplest book in what was the most comprehensive and imaginative projected series of texts in the history of education up to that time, its realization came only after a long and intense period devoted to the attempt to reform the entire process of education as it then existed.

COMENIUS: THE EARLY YEARS 1592-1627

Preparation for the Ministry

Jan Amos Komenský (1592-1670) was born in Moravia and became an orphan in early childhood. He grew up in the faith of his parents, the Unitas Fratrum (Unity of the Brethren), an Anabaptist sect that found its inspiration in the life and martyrdom of the Bohemian reformer, Jan Hus (c. 1369-1415). After a short period of instruction in a vernacular school, the young Komenský was sent to the city of Herborn in the small Protestant duchy of Nassau, north of Heidelberg, where he attended a Latin-grammar school, coming to a study of that language in his sixteenth year, much later than was customary. There, as was the practice, his name became latinized to Comenius, and for the next six years he studied in grammar school and at the universities of Herborn and Heidelberg. After some travelling in western Europe, Comenius returned to Moravia in 1614, where he taught for four years in a school conducted by the Brethren at Přerov. His studies had been directed towards preparing for a religious vocation and in 1618, upon attaining a proper age, he accepted the ministry of the church at Fulnek, remaining there for three years.

Comenius' entry into the ministry coincided with the outbreak of the Thirty Years War which marked the beginning of a long period of persecution for himself and his Church. The Kingdom of Bohemia, of which Moravia was a province, became the immediate centre of the conflict in which the Catholic forces of the Hapsburgs were opposed by those Protestant groups whose demands for religious freedom were supported by a number of princes, resisting encroachment on regional sovereignty. Although Bohemia had been under Hapsburg suzerainty in the sixteenth century, the continued fractiousness of the Protestant groups meant that their toleration had become a necessary aspect of political control.

For the hundred years following the revolt of Martin Luther in 1517, the spread of Protestantism in Europe had led to an increasing amount of freedom for fundamentalist sects, including the Unitas Fratrum. The Peace of Augsburg, signed by the Hapsburg Emperor Charles V in 1555, had encouraged national movements, including the development of educational institutions. However when it seemed in 1617 that the failing Emperor Matthias might be succeeded by an even stronger Catholic ruler, in the person of Archduke Ferdinand of Styria, the Protestant groups took alarm. The following year Ferdinand was elected and in a controversy over a matter of religious toleration, Protestant anxiety built up to the point of open rebellion in Prague on May 23rd, 1618. Three years later Ferdinand crushed the rebellion. Those leaders of the revolt who had not fled the country were executed publicly and the movement for independence was quelled. Yet so involved were the religious and political affairs of Europe that the campaign in Bohemia touched off a long war involving all of western Europe in a series of major conflicts that devastated the continent, and Germany in particular, until by the time they ended in 1648, they had created more problems than they proposed originally to settle.

Faith and Reason: Early Thoughts on Education

Within three years of assuming pastoral duties Comenius found himself a member of a proscribed religion and was forced into hiding. From 1621 to 1627 he remained in seclusion, writing in Czech in 1623 his first serious philosophical treatise *Labyrinth of the World* and its sequel, *Paradise of the Heart.*[1] Constructed in allegorical form, the

1 *Labyrint světa a ráj srdce*; (*Labyrinth of the World and Paradise of the Heart*), Ed. & trans. Count Lützow, London: Dent and Co., 1901; also, Trans. Matthew Spinka, Chicago: National Union of Czechoslovak Protestants in America, 1942.

story recounted Comenius' dawning realization of the iniquities of the world and expressed his despair and disillusion at finding human society so thoroughly corrupt. Comenius felt that corruption came from the abuse of learning. The *Labyrinth* recorded his disappointment with the scholars of his time.

The way to truth, the allegory suggested, was not through secular studies, but through Christian faith. In *Paradise of the Heart* the searching Comenius met Christ, whose love, he discovered, was man's only gain. All striving was vanity. Christ counselled that one thing alone was necessary in this life, the grace of God. The problem was a difficult one. For fifteen hundred years men had sought to reconcile the claims of faith and reason as guides to human conduct. Comenius attempted to incorporate reason in his theory; from his harmonizing of faith and reason in *Paradise of the Heart* came the basis of his future thinking and his vision of the Christian way as one of education. In man, he wrote, there is in fact "a twofold clear inward light—the light of reason and the light of faith—and both are guided by the Holy Ghost. For he who enters [upon the Christian way] must put away and renounce his reason, yet the Holy Ghost returns it to him, purified and refined. . . . Then the light of faith gleams on him so brightly that he can already see and know, not only that which is before him, but also everything that is absent and invisible."[2]

Yet Comenius was a conservative, defending the primacy of faith in a period of increasing rationalism. In his view the goal of a Christian education was to know God and His works through the direction of Christ, for "the true fountain of knowledge is the Holy Writ, and the Holy Ghost our teacher, and the purpose of all true knowledge is Christ."[3]

2 *Ibid.*, pp. 218-19.

3 *Ibid.*, pp. 248-49.

Secular scholarship without such leadership was useless, even deleterious, and on this view he based his approach to the teaching of Latin. Since learning was so commonly identified with comprehension of several languages, Comenius believed men must realize that knowledge gained through language had value only when it was illuminated by God's wisdom. For, like every useful thing, language was God's work, given to man for the purpose of understanding Him. In this earthly existence man's vocation was to reach God; the journey of the soul was an educational experience. In those early years of persecution Comenius became committed to providing a way of salvation and hope for all mankind through a program of Christian education.

THE COMENIAN VISION: UNITY OF ALL HUMAN EXPERIENCE

Comenius at Leszno 1627–1641

Protestantism was suppressed vigorously by Ferdinand. From his seclusion Comenius learned that the schools of all dissenting groups throughout Austria, Bohemia and Moravia had been placed under the authority of the Catholic Church. The Jesuits, who had been given control of the University of Prague, had become responsible in the main for the eradication of Protestant belief and for the reconversion of the conquered countries to Catholicism. The policy was pursued by all possible means: the local gentry were persuaded, the peasantry coerced, Protestant pastors and schoolmasters outlawed, and the Anabaptists put to flight. Bohemia itself was subjected to such ruthless domination by its conquerors that the countryside wasted and the towns declined both in civic activity and in population. Those Protestants still in hiding near Bohemia realized that return to their homeland was to be a long way off. With many of his fellows, Comenius moved in 1627 to relative sanctuary at Leszno in Poland, a region beyond the ambit of the conflict. There, in a community of the Unitas Fratrum, Comenius became rector of the Latin-grammar school, or gymnasium, a position he occupied for fourteen years, until 1641.

At Leszno Comenius continued his theological activities, writing religious tracts and other documents. From his dual position of pastor and rector he began to develop his educational and philosophical outlook, recording his thought in two major treatises: *Didaktika* (*Didactic*) and *Didactica Magna* (*The Great Didactic*).[4] Publication of these writings did not coincide with completion of the manuscripts. *Didaktika*, written in Czech in the period 1627–32, received but a limited circulation. It was followed between 1633 and 1638 by *Didactica Magna* in Latin which was distributed only in manuscript: the lack of enthusiasm from its early readers delayed publication for almost twenty years until a collected Latin edition of the complete educational works, *Opera Didactica Omnia*, was published in 1657 in a two-volume compilation.[5]

Education as the Way to Unity

Central to Comenius' thinking was the idea of the underlying unity of all human experience. The reality of the perceptual world he accepted as axiomatic: its interpretation was the subject of his concern. Men, and scholars particularly, were at variance in their understandings of the nature of reality, and from those disagreements the most tragic

4 An exhaustive bibliography of Comenius' writings is given in Matthew Spinka, *John Amos Comenius: That Incomparable Moravian*, Chicago: University of Chicago Press, 1943.

5 A facsimile reprint to celebrate the tercentenary of the publication was issued in 1957: *Opera Didactica Omnia*, (Two Vols.), Pragae: Academia Scientiarum Bohemslovenica. All references to *Opera Didactica Omnia* (*ODO*) are to that facsimile edition.

consequences often followed. Comenius' religious beliefs provided him with the notion that a single unified world-design was the production of God, and that the world should exhibit a unity proceeding from that design. His personal motto "All things flow spontaneously in the absence of violence"[6] indicated his outlook. Disunity and its consequent social and political disharmony, in his view, stemmed from faulty understanding, therefore the problem was one of education. He visualized a system of education which would offer a progressive illumination of the intrinsic order of reality. In the schooling of his time Comenius saw that the young were led away from such enlightenment, either because they failed to relate their experiences to adequate concepts, or because they learned by purely verbal means and acquired words before they had attained the requisite sensory experiences.

Enlightenment, then, is an important concept in understanding Comenius' theory. Following his belief in the necessary unity of the world, he felt that man secured personal fulfilment in the degree that he was able to enter into the natural order of existence. As man approached that order, or harmony, so he became part of the divine plan, thereby coming to know God, its author. The place accorded to man in that plan, therefore, was of especial significance: to explain it, Comenius incorporated the viewpoint of Aristotle that man's distinctive quality was intellect and that his vocation lay in its cultivation. Whereas other forms of life, vegetative and animal, gained fulfilment in terms of appetitive and habitual behaviour, man was endowed with reason and his proper development, then, was achieved through intellectual activity. Since man was central to God's design of the universe, his task was especially

6 *Omnia sponte fluant absit violentia rebus.*

difficult—he must seek unity with the natural order of providence while at the same time cultivating the highest levels of mental awareness.

Although Comenius' theory was inconsistent in some respects, he had established that the need of man for cultivation placed a great responsibility for formation and guidance on the school. His own position as rector required that he relate his theory to the problems of teaching. To meet the demands of conducting the gymnasium at Leszno, Comenius turned to the literature on education.

The literature available was disorganized and often poorly presented; indeed little educational writing had been produced for a thousand years. Education in medieval Europe had been sustained by a meagre body of theory, much of it encyclopedic and derivative in content and outlook. The Renaissance in fourteenth-century Italy promoted some revival of education as a new enthusiasm for the classical past extended beyond Italy into the various European kingdoms. Yet despite the variety and panoramic scope of thought in both the Greek and Latin literatures, there was very little that could serve as a practical guide in the schoolroom. The one systematic, comprehensive work on educational theory and practice was the *Education of the Orator* by Quintilian, a Roman of the first century A.D. That great treatise became the mainstay of educational thought and practice from the Renaissance to Comenius' day; it was the chief guide for the rapidly multiplying Latin-grammar schools.

Quintilian's book recommended rhetorical and grammatical training by verbal, recitative means and placed a premium on powers of memorization. The method of the catechism was common to other texts, prominent among them the brief grammar, *Ars Minor,* by the fourth century A.D. Roman professor Aelius Donatus. By the latter part of the sixteenth century the practices were virtually universal throughout the civilized regions of the Continent. In the Jesuit schools of the Catholic south of Europe, in the Lutheran schools of Germany, in the private institutions modelled on Sturm's gymnasium at Strassburg which spread into the Calvinist areas, in the church schools of England, and even in the schools of the Moravians, education was the same. Latin grammar was the foundation, the classical and patristic authors the content, piety the aim, and Quintilian the method.

The Task of Educational Reform

That background was all Comenius had available to him and he realized it was inadequate to his purposes. Upon entering his duties at the gymnasium in Leszno Comenius set to the task of remedying the deficiencies in available educational theory, although he was then unaware of their extent. For the next thirty years, from 1627 to 1657, he pursued that goal. The first step was relatively simple: to prepare a text book for use in the gymnasium. Since children frequently had little or no instruction before entering the grammar school, and usually began their education directly in Latin, the difficulties in learning were great. Consequently, brutality and coercion were part of the activities of the schoolmaster, making a violent contrast with Comenius' belief in the need for the spontaneous flow of life.

Already some scholars were aware of the inadequacy of existing methods of teaching. The Irish priest William Bateus, a professor at the Jesuit college at Salamanca, had attempted some improvements as early as 1611, producing a school book that taught Latin through the Spanish vernacular by placing the two texts in parallel columns. Entitled *Janua Linguarum* (*Gateway of Tongues*), it enjoyed wide success and was translated into several other European languages. In the same period Eilhard Lubinus (1565–1621), a well-known professor of theology and mathematics at the university in Rostock, was writing on the subject, urging a more direct and meaningful approach to teaching in schools, and of Latin in particular.[7] In Germany, Wolfgang Ratke (1571–1635) who had visited England and been influenced by Bacon's theories, was urging reform of language teaching. He too argued for a meaningful approach and suggested that children study objects first and words later.

Bateus, Lubinus and Ratke stimulated Comenius and in 1631, after several years in the writing, he published at Leszno the first of his pedagogical texts, *Janua Linguarum Reserata* (*The Gate of Tongues Unlocked*).[8] This was a simple encyclopedia of a wide variety of topics, ninety-eight in all, beginning with the origins of the earth, *De Ortu Mundi*, and ending with a section on angels, *De Angelis*. The whole work, including a short introduction and an epilogue, consisted in one hundred sections, subdivided into one thousand sentences. It was intended, as the introduction stated, for teaching Latin and whatever other languages were desired.

First Steps to Reform: Early Educational Writings

The *Janua* was immediately popular, and for the next fifty years it was the best known and probably the most widely used text in Europe. In the first twenty years of publication it was issued in as many editions, frequently in multi-language printings, some containing as many as four languages in parallel columns. The major languages of

7 See Jelinek, V. (Ed. & trans.), *The Analytical Didactic of Comenius*, Chicago: University of Chicago Press, 1953, pp. 45, 49, and *passim*.

8 The influence of the Jesuit edition was acknowledged by Comenius, *ODO*, I: 253.

Europe—English, French, German and Italian—were the most popular although Dutch, Spanish, Swedish and Flemish editions were also published. In addition there was a number of Latin-Greek editions. While London and Amsterdam were the most frequent centres for publication, copies were printed in many other cities, including Geneva, Venice, Paris, Hamburg, Danzig, Frankfurt and Prague.

The introduction to *Janua* stated as one of its basic principles the idea that thought and language proceed together.[9] Its application in *Janua* was widely appreciated, and within two years of its first publication Comenius issued a simplified version to serve as a preliminary reader. Following his metaphor of the doorway to language, the simpler text was designated a portal or vestibule, the *Vestibulum*. Also encyclopedic in content, it consisted in eight major parts, divided into sections made up of short sentences, 427 in all. Although the sentences were short and simple in construction they frequently contained difficult concepts. The first three, for example, read: "God is eternal, the earth is but temporary. The angels are immortal, man is mortal. The body is visible, the soul is invisible."

In the same period Comenius wrote *Informatorium školy mateřské* (*School of Infancy*), treating of the education of the child from its very first years. Written in Czech in 1630 and translated into German three years later, a Latin version did not appear until it was included in the collected works of 1657.[10] *School of Infancy* presented the methods by which the parents, particularly the mother, could begin the child's education. Basically the method consisted in requiring the child to observe and then repeat the appropriate words. The more abstract concepts and generalizations, such as

9 *Janua Linguarum Reserata*, Article 21, in *ODO*, I: 253.

10 The most recent translation is by E. M. Eller, *The School of Infancy*, Chapel Hill: University of North Carolina Press, 1956.

those about the nature of spiritual forces, were not given special consideration: Comenius felt they were self-evident truths that could be grasped directly by logical intuition. Comenius was never to handle that problem adequately. His theory that knowledge was derived from sensory reality did not provide any explanation of the ways in which abstractions and spiritual truths were attained.

In *School of Infancy* Comenius made clear his belief that the child was part of the natural order, possessing a nature that should develop according to certain patterns of organic growth, in some way latent. Yet in his opinion such development did not proceed by an inevitable unfolding; on the contrary, man required guidance and training, even from his earliest days.

So, while adhering to the view that the young child should be trained in morality and virtue, Comenius believed that in addition, the infant's growing mental powers needed cultivation. Offering this advice to parents, he suggested that the names of all the familiar objects of the environment, and the uses for which they exist, should be learned. Since there was no appreciation at the time that learning for the very young could be organized more fruitfully on the basis of their interests, Comenius turned to the logical division of subject-matter already employed in the traditional curriculum, suggesting that the child be acquainted with the simpler ideas in the various studies of optics, astronomy, geography, chronology, history, household affairs and politics. In the first of those studies, for example, Comenius wrote that "Of *Optics* it will suffice for children to know what is darkness, what light, [and] the difference between the more common colors."[11] Similarly, the rudiments of skill in dialectics, arithmetic, geometry and music must be grasped,

11 Eller, E. M., *Op. cit.*, p. 73.

along with the performative skills of grammar, rhetoric and poetry. Describing poetry, Comenius pointed out that its principles

> arise with the beginning of speech. As soon as a baby begins to understand words it begins to love melody and rhythm. . . . [in the third and fourth years] they learn to notice the difference between prose and measured language. . . . Their training in poetry, therefore, is simply this, that from understanding some rhymes and verses, they thereby come to know what is rhythm and poetry and what is plain speech.[12]

In *School of Infancy* the encyclopedic, logically organized approach to education of *Janua* and *Vestibulum* was applied to the child's first years. At the same time, however, Comenius began to realize increasingly that words themselves must be derived from the objects of personal experience. He was convinced that proper knowledge of the world depended on the cultivation of the senses and on an adequate relation of language to experience.

The production of *School of Infancy, Vestibulum* and *Janua* in the first six years at Leszno provided a stimulation to further thought on education. In his work so far he had begun with his religious beliefs; from them Comenius proceeded to develop an educational theory. That development became incorporated in his thinking; before long Comenius' teaching activities determined the direction of his thought and consequently influenced his religious outlook. During the period at Leszno the writing that resulted was compounded of religious belief and educational activity, both of which became blended together in his major work, *Didactica Magna* (*The Great Didactic*).

12 *Ibid.*, pp. 99-100.

Like other perceptive thinkers of the time, Comenius was sensitive to the needs for educational reform. Movements in that direction were prominent in England. At the turn of the seventeenth century Francis Bacon had propounded in *Novum Organum* his influential theory of inductive scientific thinking which was part of his vast and imaginative scheme for the complete renovation of knowledge. The ideas were accepted and helped create a mood of intellectual reform. Western Europe in the early seventeenth century became increasingly receptive to intellectual discovery, particularly in France and England where the forces of Catholic reaction were not operative. The great scientists of the seventeenth century, however, were younger than Comenius by a generation or more; their discoveries did not come until later.

The Unity of All Knowledge: Pansophism

Comenius was urging the reform of knowledge, but not in terms of basic conceptions. On the contrary Comenius accepted many of the notions of his day: his concern was with the proper ordering of knowledge as it existed. Ever convinced of the unity of the universe, he presented a rationalization of that view in a lengthy pamphlet written in the years 1634–36, published at Oxford in 1637, and reissued in London in 1639 with the title *Pansophiae Prodromus*, literally, intimations of a universal science. Already Comenius had begun to develop the idea that in nature there were no divisions, classification in his view being an artifice of man that did violence to the organic continuity of the real world. The world was all one, so too was knowledge. To achieve knowledge was to reach God; in attaining a completely unified view of all existence, corporeal and spiritual, man would fulfil his natural end. Then, of necessity would harmony and peace ensue. Such was Comenius' grand educational vision: simple, compelling, exciting. It caught the imagination of reformers and statesmen, for it was in a sense typical of its time. In the mid-seventeenth century the notion of a single, universal science, of *Pansophism*, was discussed in intellectual circles throughout Europe.

Pansophism itself was for Comenius a supremely simple concept; he had no difficulty in imagining the absolute unity of all knowledge, and believed that every element of existence was related to the totality of the others. Nor did he doubt that if those relations could be determined then demonstration itself would carry such power of persuasion that it would overcome ignorance and evil. Already in the period 1627–32 he had made a tentative elaboration of the idea in his Czech *Didaktika*, including there an outline of his projected educational scheme. The idea was developed further in the Latin *Didactica Magna*, which appeared in manuscript in 1638. This was Comenius' first systematic organization of his education plans, envisaging, in effect, the total reform of all civilization.

Didactica Magna: Education as Organic Continuity

Didactica Magna was the most important educational treatise of its century: indeed, it stands as one of the greatest of all time. It was a lengthy, closely detailed document of 193 folio pages in the Amsterdam edition of the *Opera Didactica Omnia,* where it first received publication. The title page itself indicated the tremendous sweep of its contents. It proclaimed an intention to set out a method whereby all children, with no exceptions, could be taught quickly, pleasantly and certainly, the sum of all knowledge, and at the same time be imbued with such qualities of character as would be relevant for this world and the next. Having made such a claim, Comenius set to the task of justifying it. The basis of his method was an attempt to make the two separate processes of teaching and learning proceed together, in mutual accord. The standard teaching method of Comenius' day was to reduce all matter to be taught to some formal arrangement: language was organized into grammatical categories, geometry into theorems. Once patterning was achieved, the material was taught in that order. However, since the formal patterns were arrived at by other persons, they were already remote from the child's experiences at the time of presentation, and their remoteness meant that they were difficult to understand. Teachers in their turn encouraged rote learning and valued highly the child's ability to memorize. Educational achievement was measured by how much children could remember. Qualitative considerations such as the use or meaning of what they had learned could not be entertained.

Comenius, then, turned to the growth of the child's mind and attempted to find the principles by which human mentality developed. If he could find these, and replace the formal, logical patterning of subject matter by a psychological patterning drawn from knowledge of mental development, then learning and teaching could proceed together, naturally. Comenius believed that he had discovered such a set of principles, and that in effect he had also found an identity between learning and teaching.

In his view, both stemmed from the single arch-principle of organic continuity. The all-pervasive unity of the world rested in a set of sensory percepts which in turn were integrated into a series of concepts at levels of increasing abstraction and complexity. For each of those levels there was a corresponding set of linguistic categories, ranging from simple substantives to complex propositions. The task of the educator was to identify and order those categories. Language had to be the basis of all teaching and learning since knowledge subsisted in linguistic terms and propositions. Knowledge itself could be achieved most readily if the child learned to speak and to write in terms relevant to his stages of development.

Organic continuity was the basis on which the entire argument of *The Great Didactic* depended. Comenius believed that within the child were the potentialities for development; that "everything is contained in that microcosm, man."[13] From birth to maturity, consequently, man should follow the laws of his inner development, through a sequence marked by increasing acuity of perception, as well as by improvements in physical and motor skills and in linguistic competence. All human growth followed stages—infant, child, youth, adult—indicated by corresponding patterns of behaviour. Speech, which was his chief example, likewise had four stages: babbling (*quo modo cumque*), correctness (*proprie*), taste (*eleganter*), vigour (*nervose*).[14] Knowledge, therefore, should be organized to correspond to those stages: the babbling child should learn to speak simple words and phrases, the young child sentences, the youth to discourse at greater length, and the adult to achieve thereby access to the world of scholarly and classical writing. For Comenius, it is important to note, speech was not distinguished from reading; it was linked in some sort of continuous relationship. Man's earthly progress was, then, one of progressive refinement, of qualitative changes in perception and understanding. The growth of the intellect was marked by changes in degree, not in kind. From infancy throughout life the totality of knowledge was to be pursued at increasing levels of sophistication; as man grew in knowledge so he grew towards God.

13 *Homini utpote* μικροκόσμῳ *omnia inesse, Didactica Magna,* XIX: V, 41, in *ODO*, I: p. 109.

14 *Ibid.*, XXII: VI, 14, *ODO*, I: p. 129.

From that position Comenius developed a curriculum, and in doing so drew from his earlier experiences in writing *School of Infancy, Vestibulum* and *Janua*. From infancy to adulthood, the individual should be concerned with the totality of experience, the progressive cultivation of the intellect should stem from the discovery of ever-increasing meaning in experience. Knowledge became enriched with the finding of new and fresh relationships in existing situations.

Ideal of the Graded Series of Pansophic Texts

Comenius turned in *The Great Didactic* to the formal organization of studies. Since man needed training and cultivation to achieve his vocation, then institutions had to be provided, of which a system of graded schools and a series of graded text books were of the greatest significance. In place of the variety of unrelated institutions of his day, Comenius wanted to articulate a program of formal studies. The four stages of linguistic development were related to a set of schools: that of the mother's lap (*Gremium maternum*), the public vernacular school (*Schola Vernacula publica*), the Latin-grammar school or gymnasium (*Schola Latina*), and the university followed by travel (*Academia et Peregrinationes*).[15] His suggestions for pre-school instruction had been expressed in *School of Infancy*; little beyond recapitulation appeared in *The Great Didactic.* Development of the same studies as outlined in the *School of Infancy* continued in the vernacular school, although Comenius never wrote on that institution in any detail, probably because he was so deeply concerned with Latin.

The Latin-grammar school was ever the centre of his interests, and in *The Great Didactic* he discussed its reform

15 *Ibid.,* XXVII, 2, *ODO,* I: p. 165.

at length. In his view, its curriculum should deal with all knowledge, but at increasingly abstract levels. Intended for young people between the ages of twelve and eighteen, its studies were to be based upon six formal disciplines of grammar, dialectics, rhetoric, ethics, physics and mathematics. Possession of Latin was of great importance for through it all scholarship proceeded.

For the grammar school Comenius planned a set of graded text books employing the principles already applied in *Vestibulum* and *Janua.* Following the metaphor used by Bateus in *Gateway of Tongues* Comenius chose titles to correspond with the features of Roman classical architecture. The increasing difficulty of the texts was symbolized by the student's movement into the "house of learning". By the progressive cultivation of the Latin language the young person could proceed from the vestibule, through the doorway into the courtyard, thence into the palace of knowledge, there to find in the works of the great authors man's real earthly treasure.

In *The Great Didactic* the sequence was foreshadowed: to *Vestibulum* and *Janua* were added *Atrium* (Courtyard), *Palatium* (Palace), *Thesaurus* (Treasury). The plan, however, remained undeveloped. A beginning was made several years later with an *Atrium*, but it did not achieve any widespread application. The *Palatium and Thesaurus*, designed as readings from classical authors, were never written.

Comenius did not pursue the question of academic studies and wrote very little about the university.[16] It seems reasonably certain, however, that he intended the university to be occupied with the cultivation of all knowledge at the highest possible level. He was concerned particularly with the clear

16 The most relevant of Comenius' writings on the subject have been collected by R. F. Young, *Comenius in England*, London: Oxford University Press, 1932.

expression of ideas, feeling that responsibility in this respect had to be accepted by the scholarly community. To deal with that specific problem he suggested the establishment of an institution which would form, at the same time, the apex of his system of education. This was the College of Light, or Pansophic College, about which he wrote in some detail.

Institutions of advanced learning were being established in Europe at that time. The French Academy had been founded in 1635, preceded by two of less importance at Rome and Florence. In 1641 Comenius travelled to London at the invitation of a friend, Samuel Hartlib, to present to the English parliament his proposals for a College of Light. However, the parliament was in recess; when it reconvened it was preoccupied with the Irish insurrection and the tensions of the impending civil war. Comenius' proposals were never given a public hearing, although his influence contributed to the formation in 1660 of the Royal Society, an English association devoted to the advance of scientific knowledge. His ideas on the subject were recorded in a document written during his London visit of 1641 and first published in Amsterdam in 1668 as *Via Lucis* (*The Way of Light*).[17]

The primary concern of the College of Light, Comenius suggested, was the organization of knowledge in such a way that it could be made readily available to all persons. That in turn raised the issue of communication. Despite the universality of Latin in the scholarly world, Comenius considered it to be inadequate to the task. The pressing need, in his view, was for a new, truly universal language. He believed that one could be devised to avoid the syntactical and semantic difficulties of Latin, and so to act as a universal antidote to confusion of thought. The ideal language should

17 The standard English translation is E. T. Campagnac, *The Way of Light*, Liverpool: The University Press, 1938.

be thoroughly rational and logical, and correspond completely to the objects of experience. It would, consequently, be easier and more pleasant to learn. Comenius recognized the many difficulties in the way of such a project, however, and he was realistic enough to know that he would have to settle for Latin.

Two Further Efforts at Reform: Sweden and Transylvania 1642–54

After the failure of his mission in England, Comenius accepted an invitation to help with the improvement of the Swedish schools, chiefly by writing text books. In 1642, with some misgivings about the project, he left for the Baltic town of Elbing. There, for the following six years, until July, 1648, he continued his work of educational reform.

At Elbing Comenius wrote his third major educational treatise, *Linguarum Methodus Novissima*, which contained the most mature expression of his educational thought. The tenth chapter, translated and published by later scholars under the separate title of *Didaktika Analytická* (*Analytical Didactic*),[18] was his third didactic work. He urged the use of the vernacular along with Latin, for their mutual clarification, and the inclusion of occasional pictorial illustrations. The writing of the complete work was hindered by the increasingly irksome task of preparing school texts although by 1648 he had made reasonable progress.

In that year Comenius was elected Bishop of the Unitas Fratrum and he moved to Leszno. In 1648, also, the Thirty Years War was concluded by the Treaty of Westphalia. Disappointed greatly by the fact that the Treaty gave no recognition to his Church, Comenius moved yet again to the security of Sáros-Pátak in the independent Hungarian state

18 Jelinek, V., *Op. cit.*, p. 3 ff.

of Transylvania. There he pursued his dream of universal peace, and worked at the reform of its school system. It was there that he conceived and first drafted the book for which he was to be remembered chiefly in the following two hundred years: *Orbis Sensualium Pictus.*

The Final Years: Leszno and Amsterdam 1654–70

Comenius remained in Sáros-Pátak for six years and then, in 1654, returned to Leszno. His return was marked by personal tragedy. Within a year war broke out between Sweden and Poland over the latter's refusal to recognize some of Sweden's gains from the Thirty Years War. In 1656 the Swedes overran Poland and Leszno suffered destruction. Comenius lost all of his personal belongings, including a precious twenty-year accumulation of unpublished manuscripts. He fled to Amsterdam where, under the patronage of the de Geer family, he lived for the remaining fourteen years of his life, still writing indefatigably. It was from Amsterdam that he directed the publication of *Orbis Pictus.*

ORBIS SENSUALIUM PICTUS

During the years 1653 and 1654 Comenius outlined the general idea that was to become *Orbis Pictus* in a single page, published subsequently in *Opera Didactica Omnia.* In that brief statement he set out the features of the new project. Since it was his belief that nothing entered the intellect except through the senses, and that all learning depended on a prior basis in adequate perceptual experiences, so he felt that a new aid to schooling was demanded (*En igitur novum Scholis subsidium!*). That aid, he announced, was to be a small book, encyclopedic in scope, with the content organized around pictures of objects accompanied by their names and verbal descriptions. The *Janua,* already well known, was to be the basis. To show how it might be adapted to the new project, Comenius gave an example:

Exempli gratia,

Mun-dus.

(Picta Tabella.)

Deus (1) creavit Mundum.
Coelum habet (2) *Stellas,*
Nubes (3) pendent in Aëre
Aves (4) volant sub Nubibus.
Pisces (5) natant in Aqua.
Terra habet *Montes* (6) & *Sylvas* (7)
& *Campos* (8) et *Animalia* (9) *Hominesq*; (10) etc.

Some of these phrases were later transferred without modification to *Orbis Pictus*, with the addition of an appropriate picture above each set of information.

Development of Illustrated Books for Children

It was the introduction of illustrations that was to make *Orbis Pictus* unique in the history of school text books. The idea was not altogether new. As early as 1617 Lubinus had suggested that languages should be studied through books with short sentences accompanied by illustrations.[19] He was aware that, despite the widespread employment of printing and the public acceptance of books, there was little application of those resources to school use beyond the straightforward production of grammars and dictionaries. Lubinus' notion of illustrating a school book represented a significant departure from the customary attitude to school learning. Comenius, however, was comparatively slow to realize the possibilities, even though as early as 1630 he had written in *School of Infancy* that children should learn in part by experience, since pictures "in books and on walls please

19 *Ibid.*, p. 87.

them, so they ought not to be denied; rather, one ought to take pains to provide and point out such things to them."[20]

The elements of the new conception were already in existence. Both Lubinus and Comenius were conversant with a variety of illustrated books including encyclopedias which had been in wide circulation among European scholars for more than a century. The earliest of these were the block-books of the fifteenth century which copied medieval manuscript format with the significant departure that the illustrations and text for each page were cut together on a single block of wood. At the same time numerous publications were employing the convention of putting labels or passages of conversation on banners or streamers near the figures of persons speaking. Encyclopedias and compendia, proving both popular and profitable, were printed at many locations and exhibited a variety of approaches. By the end of the fifteenth century the illustrated, labelled encyclopedia was well established, exemplified in such notable productions as Bartholemaeus' *All the Proprytees of Thynges* (1495) and Gregor Reisch's *Margarita Philosophica* (1496).

Illustrated books for children, however, were not so common. School texts were virtually non-existent in classical and medieval times, due to the difficulties of producing many copies. Multiple production of school texts had been made possible by the development of the block-book in the fifteenth century, and shortly afterwards school books, mostly grammars, were printed by means of the new invention of movable type. Yet such products did no more than follow the customary pattern and remained unillustrated.

By the year 1500 the printing of traditional school grammars had become a staple of the printing trade. The well-

20 Eller, E. M., *Op. cit.*, p. 87.

known German printer Wynkyn de Worde, who established his press in London at the beginning of the sixteenth century, devoted forty per cent of his production to school grammars and depended on their profits for the success of his business as a whole.[21] The position was similar on the Continent: Gutenberg issued twenty-four editions of *Ars Minor*, and other printers rivalled his output. One Cologne printer issued twenty Latin grammars and dictionaries in a four-year period.[22]

Some illustrated books for children made their appearance in the same period but they were not meant for school use, being intended either for private religious devotions (primers), for edification, or even for diversion. One of the most popular was Caxton's 1484 edition of Aesop's *Fables*, illustrated with 185 woodcuts containing captions. There were others, on similar moralistic and didactic lines, but none designed for the classroom.

When the first illustrated school text, *Orbis Pictus*, appeared in 1658, its influence was increased by the fact that it represented the culmination of efforts of the most persistent and well-known text-book writer of the century. After forty years of unremitting attention to the process of education, in which practical experience as master and rector were significant features, Comenius brought together in *Orbis Pictus* an expression of the many separate notions that had occupied his thoughts.

His pedagogical principles of learning by doing, of beginning with simple concrete experiences and seeing the whole world as a classroom could not be put into general effect without the use of books.

21 Steinberg, S., *Five Hundred Years of Printing*, Harmondsworth: Penguin, 1955, p. 72.

22 *Ibid.*, p. 100.

Comenius was aware of the importance of the written word. All of his educational endeavours had been directed towards developing a graded curriculum whereby the child could come progressively into increased mastery of language, which he saw as the means whereby knowledge was symbolized and made relevant. Symbols, Comenius recognized, were themselves abstractions from reality. Words came from the experiences of life which, if inaccessible to direct encounter could be mediated through such verbal symbols.

The implementation of that discovery in *Orbis Pictus* was Comenius' triumph. The fact that he did not study further the many relationships between words and the experiences they symbolize does not detract from his achievement. For the first time in the history of Western education a text book attempted to make the symbolic abstractions of language meaningful to the schoolchild in terms of personal experience.

Seventeenth-century schoolchildren had to study in two languages, the universal Latin and the vernacular. By that time the vernaculars had become well developed for all of the needs of daily life and children learnt them first. Yet all serious learning was preserved in Latin; it was the language of the professions and the law courts. Since Latin was approached by children as a foreign language, there was an even greater need to make it as meaningful as possible. Comenius sought to introduce greater vividness and reality through the use of an illustrated reader in which the vernacular and Latin proceeded together.

By 1654 Comenius had simplified the text of *Janua*, which, with the addition of illustrations, was to be his new Latin reader. From Saros-Pátak Comenius wrote a short note to the effect that neither a suitable artist nor an adequate printer was to be found in Hungary. In that same year, 1654, Comenius left for those two tragic years in Leszno and the manuscript was sent to Nuremberg, an important centre of book production, and entrusted to the publisher, Michael Ender. Four years later, in 1658, from his relatively settled location in Amsterdam, Comenius saw *Orbis Pictus* issued in its first edition in the two languages of Latin and German.[23]

First Edition of Orbis Pictus: *Nuremberg, 1658*

In the first edition the text was set in parallel columns, Latin on the left, German on the right. Both columns were extremely close in content although at times they diverged slightly. Accompanying each of the 150 chapters of the book was a woodcut illustration in black and white, with numbers indicating objects mentioned in the text. The illustrations were small, averaging $3\frac{1}{2}$ by $2\frac{1}{2}$ inches. The individual strokes of the graver were firm and distinct, and the design exhibited the influence of the calligraphic tradition of German woodcut in contrast to the styles of Italy, France and the Netherlands where finer gradations and suggestions of tone were characteristic.

The typography itself was arresting, and included an unusual combination of typefaces. The Latin text was set in the customary roman face: lower case and capitals. Words corresponding to the objects numbered in the illustration were printed in italics followed immediately by their respective numbers, the text reading in numerical sequence. For the German, only black-letter type (known also as Fraktur and Old English) was used, the specially numbered words being emphasized in a bolder face. Thus each page was set in four separate faces—roman, italic, black-letter, black-letter bold—and this was something of a typographical innovation. Certainly the use of such techniques of visual emphasis in a school book was a considerable development.

23 This edition is now extremely rare. A copy is held in the Bibliothèque Nationale, Paris.

The content itself followed that already elaborated in the many editions of *Janua* and reflected much prevailing belief. Although the physical format of *Orbis Pictus* was experimental, even revolutionary, and its pedagogical principles equally innovatory, its approach to knowledge was strongly traditional. Such resistance to change was not unusual in a school book, but some of the omissions in his encyclopedia were made conspicuous by the fact that Comenius was living at a time of great discoveries. The geocentric theory of the universe was being replaced by the heliocentric theory proposed by Copernicus (1473–1543) and developed further by Galilei (1564–1642). The world had been circumnavigated and explored, the voyages of Tasman in 1642 and 1644 having added the new continent of "Terra Australis" to the charts of Dutch mapmakers. Harvey (1578–1657) had established the circulatory theory of the blood by 1628. None of these advances, however, was recorded in the first edition of *Orbis Pictus.* Instead Comenius stated that the heavens rotated around the earth, that in the southern hemisphere was the unknown land, that the veins carried blood to the body from the liver and the arteries carried heat and warmth from the heart.

Those three examples indicate the entire conception around which the book was constructed, the belief that knowledge could be ordered objectively and kept constant. Such an outlook was not compatible with continual discovery. Schoolmasters, however, did not see any problem. *Orbis Pictus* was an immediate success, and in the following year was printed in London.

First English Edition: London, 1659

The first English edition of *Orbis Pictus* was a close copy of the Nuremberg publication; in general, the Latin text remained the same, although in places there were slight syntactical rearrangements. The English text was prepared by Charles Hoole, a London schoolmaster. The title-page did not indicate clearly which language was used as the basis for the English translation. It stated simply that the book was "written by the Author in Latine and High-Dutch . . . and translated into English . . . for the use of Young Latin scholars." The term High-Dutch was apparently a mistranslation of *Hoch Deutsch* (*High German*). In his preliminary remarks, however, Hoole pointed out that he had avoided translating the German text as it contained idiomatic expressions unsuited to English children.

Two major changes marked the English edition: the order of the text was reversed to place English first, and the woodcuts were replaced by copper engravings. Since copper plates give impressions that are almost indistinguishable from woodcuts, the illustrations appeared to be unchanged. The content itself was printed in a style similar to that of the Nuremberg edition, the Latin was set in roman and italic faces, the English in black-letter, with emphasized words indicated by a roman face. The employment of black-letter for the English text deserves comment. Black-letter had already begun to decline in England in the early seventeenth century and by 1659 it was virtually obsolete, having been replaced by roman founts even for theological books. Its use in the first and several subsequent editions of *Orbis Pictus* is therefore unusual; doubtless its employment reflected the theological conservatism of the religious grammar schools where the book was used chiefly. It must also be explained in part by the continued disinclination of printers to lavish their most advanced techniques on school books.

School Book Editions of Orbis Pictus, *1659–1845*

The book was so well received that it was repeated in numerous editions, at first in rapid succession; then in the eighteenth century at longer intervals. Many editions were nothing more than reprintings from former plates, and they should properly be called impressions. However, *Orbis Pictus* appeared in numerous genuine editions in which the text was emended, occasionally updated, and reset in new type. The illustrations too were changed in various editions, in general reflecting increasing sensitivity to the demands of school book illustration.

Orbis Pictus initiated a tradition in school text books, designed to be put in the hands of the children themselves. Its example was followed enthusiastically and throughout the eighteenth century large numbers of illustrated texts appeared, all reflecting its influence.

Further German editions were published in close succession: 1659, 1662, 1668, 1669, 1678. The position was similar in England where editions were issued in 1664, 1668, 1672 and 1685. In addition, three multi-language versions were published: one from Bratislava in 1667 in Latin, French, German and Polish; another at Nuremberg a year earlier in 1666 in Latin, French, German and Italian, and the latter was reissued thirteen years later in 1679. Throughout the eighteenth century further editions were printed, chiefly in Nuremberg and London. It is known that copies were printed also in Moscow, 1768; Vienna, 1776, 1780; Leipzig, 1784; St. Petersburg, 1808; New York, 1810; Reutlingen, 1835, 1836, 1837, 1838 and 1842; and finally Prague, 1845.

Changes occurred in the later editions of *Orbis Pictus*, although more was conserved than was altered. In the English editions of the eighteenth century the black-letter was replaced by roman type and in most of them the text was made to correspond as closely as possible in parallel columns. In the German editions especially the engravings reached extremely high levels of technical competence, those in the Reutlingen issues being steel engravings of excellent graphic quality, although they reflected the prevailing lack of aesthetic attraction.

It is the absence of change in the content that compels attention. In all editions published up to the end of the eighteenth century the content in respect to the sciences remained pre-Copernican, and the Galenic physiology continued to teach that the liver distributed blood to the body through the veins. Not until the New York reprinting in 1810 of the twelfth London edition were any significant departures made. In the American version, the section on the circulation of the blood was revised although the geocentric universe and the sixteenth-century map of the world remained unchanged. The editor included two sections of his own, one on botany, another on the Deluge in which he stated that the great flood disturbed the earth, broke up mountains and gouged out valleys, dredging up sea shells from the ocean floor and depositing them from the tops of the highest mountains to the most inland regions.

The German editions were the most changed. The German-Latin edition of 1746 from Nuremberg employed new illustrations, and added an equally comprehensive second part.

The last significant printing of *Orbis Pictus*, retitled *Neuer Orbis Pictus für die Jugend* (*A New Orbis Pictus for Children*), came in a series of four impressions: 1835, 1836, 1837 and 1838, from Reutlingen, in the four-language text of Latin, German, French and English. A final edition from the same series, which included Italian, was issued in 1842. The text was rewritten completely and brought up to date: "The golden sun, shining serenely and continually in the heavens, warms and illumines the earth which revolves around it." The illustrations were engraved expertly in steel plates, the typography and presswork were of uniformly high standard; it represented the finalization of the conception. Nothing more was possible.

The last school edition was printed, rather appropriately, in Czech along with German, French and Latin, at Prague in 1845. It was a superior production, its typographic and illustrative quality rivalled the editions from Reutlingen. Yet, curiously, the content was not so improved. The same description of the earth as that used in 1658 was retained: "The heavens rotate around the earth which stands in the centre," and although a modification was added: "as earlier men believed, at present it is thought that the earth moves around the sun," the ambiguity remained. It betrayed an indecision of intention, in contrast to the firm statement of the Reutlingen version several years previously. Furthermore, a certain regression was evident with Australia again designated as the unknown land. Perhaps in that final printing from Comenius' homeland there was a hint of the original conception, the desperate wish to hold still a changing world, to reduce it to a formal, structural pattern and transmit it to all persons so that all activities on this earth might proceed smoothly, unhindered by violence.

First Multi-Language Edition

The first five editions of *Orbis Pictus* were bi-lingual, in German (1658, 1659, 1662), and English (1659, 1664). In 1666 the first multi-lingual edition appeared, published at Nuremberg in German, Latin, Italian and French, and from which the following facsimile pages were taken: pages 320 and 321 from chapter LXXXIV, including the illustration of the wagon.

LXXXIV.

Die Wägen. Vehicula.

Mit dem Schlitten 1	*Trahâ* 1	Traha, f. 1. der Schlitte.
fahren wir	vehimur	Véhere, 2. 3. fahren.
über Schnee	super *nivibus*	Nix, f. 3. der Schnee.
und Eis.	& *glacie*.	Glacies, f. 5. das Eis.
Ein Wagen mit einem Rad	*Vehiculum unirotum* n. 2.	
wird genannt	dicitur	
ein Schubkarre; 2	*pabo*; 2 m. 3.	
mit zweyen Rädern	*birotum* n. 2.	
ein Karre; 3	*Carrus*; 3 m. 2.	
mit vieren	*quadrirotum* n. 2.	
ein Wagen,	*currus*, m. 4.	
welcher	qui	

LXXXIV.

Syr. Cap. XXXIII. Vers. 5.

Deß Narren Hertz ist wie ein Rad am Wagen; und seine Gedanken lauffen um/wie die Nabe.

Præcordia fatui, quasi rota carri; & quasi axis versatilis cogitatus illius.

L' interióre d' uno stolto è, come la ruóta d' un carro; ed i suói discorsi sono, come un perno che gira.

Le dedans du fol est comme le tour d' une rouë; & ses discours, comme l' aisseau de la roue, qui tourne.

J Carri.	*Les Chariots.*
Noi ci lisciámo	Sur la neige
in tréggia, 1 *liscia*	& glace
sopra la neue,	nous nous trainons, *glissons*
e 'l ghiáccio.	en traineau. 1
Una carrióla da una ruóta sola,	C' est
s' addimanda	une broüette, 2
carretta da bráccia; 2	qu' une cariole à une rouë;
da due ruóte,	Carrette, 3
Carretto; 3	qu' à deux rouës;
da quatro poi	mais à quatre,
un carro,	un char,
che serue	qui sert

Second Multi-Language Edition

The second multi-lingual edition appeared in 1667. It was published in Wratislava in Latin, French, German and Polish and from it the following facsimile pages were taken: pages 86 and 87 from chapter xxxvii, *The External Parts of Man.*

XXXVII.	XXXVII.
Membra Hómi-nis Externa.	**Les Membres exterieurs de l'homme.**
Caput 1 est suprà;	La *Teste* 1 est au dessus;
infrà, *Pedes*. 20	les *pieds* en bas 20
Colli	La *partie anterieure*
(quod définit	du *col*
in *Axillas* 2	qui se termine
pars ánterior,	aux *espaules*, 2
est *júgulum*: 3	est la gorge: 3 (gosier)
posterior,	celle de derniere
Cervix. 4	le *chinon*. 4
Pectus, 5	La *Poictrine*, 5
est antè;	est par deuant,
retrò, *Dorsum*: 6	le *dos* par derriere: 6
in illo,	en icelle
sunt *fœminis*,	les *femmes* ont,
binæ *Mammæ* 7	deux *mammelles* 7
cum *Papillis*.	auec Leurs *bouts*. (tetins)
Sub pectore,	sous la poitrine
est *Venter*; 9	est le *ventre*; 9
in ejus *medio*,	au *milieu* d'iceluy
Vmbilícus; 10	le *nombril*; 10
subtus *Inguen*, 11	sous l'*eine* 11
& *pudenda*.	les parties honteuses;
A tergo,	par *derriere*,

sunt

XXXVII.

Die äusserlichen Glieder des Menschen.

Das Haupt 1 ist oben;
unten/die Füsse. 20
Des Halses
(der sich endet
an den Achseln 2
Vördertheil/
ist die Kähle: 3
das Hintertheil/
der Nacken 4
Die Brust/ 5
ist vornen;
hinten/der Rucken: 6
an jener/
haben die Weibsbilder/
zwo Dutten (Brüste) 7
mit Warzen (Zitzen.)
Unter der Brust/
ist der Bauch; 9
in dessen Mitte/
der Nabel; 10
darunter der Schmerbauch/ 11
und die Scham.
Auf dem Rücken/

XXXVII.

Członki człowiecze powierzchne.

Głowá 1 jest ná wierzchu;
ná spodku/ Nogi. 20
Szyje
(ktora się kończy
ná Páchách 2)
przednia część/
jest podgárdłek: 3
tylna [(przodek szyje)
Kark. 4
Piers/ 5
jest ná przodku;
ná zádzie/ Grzebit: 6
ná oney/
białe głowy máją/
dwá Cycki/ 7
z Brodawkámi.
Pod piersią
jest Brzuch; 9
ná tego po śrzodku
Pępek; 10
podnim Łono/ (niska
[część brzucha) 11
y Członki wstydliwe:
Ná Grzbiecie

Das Ringel-Rennen.

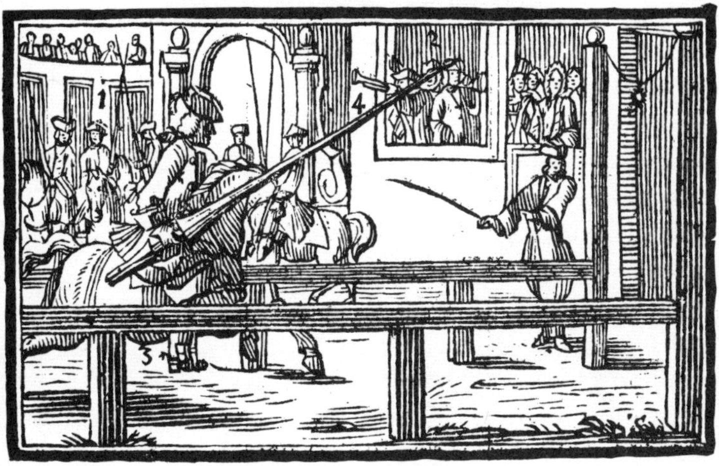

EXTENSION OF CONTENT

In the 1746 Nuremberg edition a second part was added, equal in length to the traditional first part of *Orbis Pictus.* The second dealt with new subjects, as this illustration from chapter v, *Equestrian Manoeuvres,* shows.

A LATER VERSION OF *Orbis Pictus*

The actual size illustration at left comes from chapter xxxvii, *The External Parts of Man*, in the Latin/German edition of 1746, published at Nuremberg. In this version the illustrations were much improved and the size of the pages was enlarged considerably.

EDITOR'S NOTE

Only in some printings of this edition was Charles Hoole's preface to the first edition included, which is reproduced here.

In imposing the facsimile pages for this modern printing, several errors of imposition in the original edition were discovered. They are: (i) folio 166 has been given as 199, (ii) page 175 comes before page 174, and (iii) folio 221 is repeated and folio 223 omitted. In these instances, the correct page numbers appear in the indexes.

FACSIMILE OF

THE THIRD LONDON EDITION, 1672

IOHAN-AMOS COMENIVS,
MORAUVS A°. ÆTAT 50: 1642.
T. Croß Sculpsit

JOH. AMOS COMMENII

ORBIS

SENSUALIUM

PICTUS:

Hoc est,
Omnium fundamentalium in Mundo Rerum, & in vitâ Actionum, Pictura & Nomenclatura.

JOH. AMOS COMMENIUS's

VISIBLE

WORLD:

OR,

A *Picture* and *Nomenclature* of all the chief Things that are in the World; and of Mens Employments therein.

A Work newly written by the Author in Latine and High-Dutch (being one of his last *Essays*, and the most suitable to Childrens capacities of any that he hath hitherto made) and translated into English,

By *CHARLES HOOLE*, M. A.

For the Use of Young Latine-Scholars.

Nihil est in intellectu, quod non prius fuit in sensu. Arist.

LONDON,
Printed by *T. R.* for *S. Mearne*, Book-binder to the Kings most Excellent Majesty, 1672.

2 *Gen.* 19, 20.

The Lord God brought unto *Adam* every Beaſt of the Field, and every Fowl of the Air, to ſee what he would call them. And *Adam* gave Names to all Cattel, and to the Fowl of the Air, and to every Beaſt of the Field.

2 Gen. 19, 20.

Adduxit Dominus Deus ad Adam *cunctas Animantias Terræ, & univerſa volatilia Cœli, ut videret quomodo vocaret illa. Appellavitque* Adam *Nominibus ſuis cuncta Animantia, & univerſa volatilia Cœli, & omnes Beſtias Agri.*

THE
Authors *PREFACE* TO THE
READER.

INstruction *is the means to expel Rudeness*, with which young Wits ought to be well-furbished in Schools: But so, as that the Teaching be 1. *True*, 2. *Full*, 3. *Clear*, and 4. *Solid*.

1. It will be *true*, if nothing be taught but such as are beneficial to ones life; least there be a cause of complaining afterwards. We know not necessary things, because we have not learned things necessary.

2. It will be *full*, if the mind be polished for Wisdom, the Tongue for Eloquence, and the Hands for a neat way of Living. This will be that *Grace* of ones life, *to be wise, to act, to speak.*

3.4. It will be *clear*, and by that firm and *solid*, if whatever is taught and learned, be not obscure, or confused, but apparent, distinct, and articulate, as the fingers on the hands.

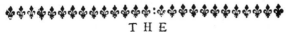

The ground of this business, is, that *sensual objects be rightly presented to the senses*, for fear they may not be received. I say, and say it again aloud, that this last is the foundation of all the rest: because *we can neither act nor speak wisely, unless we first rightly understand all the things which are to be done, and whereof, we are to speak. Now there is nothing in the understanding which was not before in the sense. And therefore to exercise the senses well about the right perceiving the differences of things, will be to lay the grounds for all wisdom, and all wise discourse, and all*

discreet actions in ones course of life. Which, because it is commonly neglected in Schools, and the things that are to be learned are offered to Scholars, without being understood, or being rightly presented to the senses, it cometh to pass, that the work of teaching and learning goeth heavily onward, and affordeth little benefit.

See here then a new help for Schools, *A Picture and Nomenclature of all the chief things in the World, and of mens Actions in their way of living!* Which, that you, good Masters, may not be loth to run over with your Scholars, I will tell you in short, what good you may expect from it.

It is *a little Book*, as you see, of no great bulk, yet a brief of the whole world, and a whole language: *full of Pictures, Nomenclatures, and Descriptions of things.*

I. *The Pictures* are the Representations of all visible things, (to which also things invisible are reduced after their fashion) of the whole world. And that in that very order of things, in which they are described in the *Janua Latinæ Linguæ* and with that fulness, that nothing very necessary or of great concernment is omitted.

II. *The Nomenclatures* are the Inscriptions, or Titles set every one over their own Pictures, expressing the whole thing by its own general Term.

III. *The Descriptions* are the Explications of the Parts of the Picture, so expressed by their own proper terms, as that same Figure which is added to every piece of the Picture, and the term of it, always sheweth what things belongeth one to another.

Which such Book, and in such a dress may (I hope) serve,

I. *To entice witty Children to it*, that they may not conceit a torment to be in the School, but dainty-fare. For it is apparent, that Children (even from their Infancy almost) are delighted with Pictures, & willingly please their eys with these sights: And it will be very well worth the pains to have once brought it to pass, that scarcrows may be taken away out of wisdoms Gardens.

II. This same little Book will serve *to stir up the Attention, which is to be fastned upon things, and ever to be sharpned more and more*; which is also a great matter. For the senses (being the main guids of Child-hood, because therein the mind doth not as yet raise up it self to an abstracted contemplation of things) evermore seek their own objects, and if they be away, they grow dull, and wry themselves hither and thither, out of a weariness of themselves: but when their objects are present, they grow merry, wax lively, and willingly suffer themselves to be fastened upon them, till the thing be sufficiently discerned. This Book then will do a good piece of service in taking (especially flickering) Wits and preparing them for deeper studies.

III. Whence a third good will follow, that *Children being won hereunto, and drawn over with this way of heeding, may be furnished with the knowledge of the Prime things that are in the world, by sport, and merry pastime.* In a word, this Book will serve for the more pleasing using of *the Vestibulum, and Janua Linguarum*, for which end it was even at the first chiefly intended. Yet if it like any that it be bound up in their native tongues also, it promiseth three other good things of it self.

I. First *it will afford a devise for learning to read, more easily than hitherto*; especially having *a Symbolical Alphabet* set before it, to wit, the Characters of the several Letters, with the Image of that creature, whose voyce that Letter goeth about to imitate, pictured by it. For the young A b c Scholar will easily remember the force of every Character by the very looking upon the Creature, till the imagination being strengthened by use can readily afford all things, and then having looked over *a Table of the chief Sillables* also (which yet was not thought necessary to be added to this Book) he may proceed to the viewing of the Pictures, and the Inscriptions set over them. Where again the very looking upon the thing pictured suggesting the name of the thing, will tell him how the Title of the Picture is to be read. And thus the whole Book being gone over by the bare Titles of the Pictures, Reading cannot but be learned; and indeed too, which thing is to be noted, *without using any ordinary tedious spelling, that most troublesome torture of wits*, which may wholly be avoided by this Method. For the often reading over the Book, by those larger Descriptions of things, and which are set after the Pictures, will be able perfectly to beget a habit of reading.

II. The same Book *being used in English in English Schools, will serve for the perfect learning of the whole English tongue, and that from the bottom*; because by the aforesaid Descriptions of things, the words and Phrases of the whole language are found set orderly in their own places. And a short English Grammar might be added at the end; clearly resolving the Speech already understood into its parts

parts, ſhewing the declining of the ſeveral words,and reducing thoſe that are joyned together under certain Rules.

III.Thence a new benefit cometh,that *that very Engliſh tranſlation,may ſerve for the more ready and pleaſant learning of the Latin tongue:* as one may ſee in this Edition,the whole Book being ſo tranſlated,that every where one word anſwereth to the word over againſt it,and the Book is in all things the ſame,only in two idiomes, as a man clad in a double garment. And there might be alſo ſome Obſervations and Advertiſements added in the end,touching thoſe things only,wherein the uſe of the Latin tongue differeth from the Engliſh. For,where there is no difference, there needeth no advertiſement to be given. But,becauſe *the firſt tasks of Learners ought to be little,and ſingle,* we have filled this firſt Book of training one up to ſee a thing of himſelf with nothing but Rudiments, that is, with the chief of things and words or with the grounds of the whole world, and the whole language, and of all our Underſtanding about things. If a more perfect Deſcription of things and a fuller knowledge of a language,and a clearer light of the underſtanding be ſought after(as they ought to be) they are to be found ſome where elſewhither there will now be an eaſie paſſage by this our *little Encyclopadia* of things ſubject to the ſenſes: Something remaineth to be ſaid touching the more cheerful uſe of this Book.

I. Let it be given to children into their hands to delight themſelves withall as they pleaſe,with the ſight of the pictures,and making them as familiar to themſelves as may be, and that even at home,before they be put to School. II. Then

II. Then let them be examined ever and anon (especially now in the School) what this thing or that thing is, and is called, so that they may see nothing, which they know not how to name, and that they can name nothing, which they cannot shew.

III. And let the things named them be shewed, not only in the Picture, but *also* in themselves; for example, the parts of the Body, Clothes, Books, the House, Utensils, *&c.*

IV. Let them be suffered also to imitate the Pictures by hand, if they will, nay rather, let them be encouraged, that they may be willing: first thus to quicken the attention also towards the things; and to observe the proportion of the parts one towards another; and lastly, to practise the nimbleness of the hand, which is good for many things.

V If any things here mentioned, cannot be presented to the eye, it will be to no purpose at all, to offer them by themselves to the Scholars, as, colours; relishes, *&c.* which cannot here be pictured out with Ink. For which reason it were to be wished, that things rare and not easie to be met withall at home, might be kept ready in every great School, that they may be shewed also, as often as any words are to be made of them, to the Scholars.

Thus at the last this School would indeed become a School of things obvious to the senses, and an Entrance to the School Intellectual. But enough: let us come to the thing it self.

The Translator to all judicious, and industrious School-Masters.

Gentlemen,

THere are few of you (I think) but have seen, and with great willingness made use of, or at least perused,) many of the Books of this well deserving Author Mr. John Commenius, which, for their profitableness to the speedy attainment of a Language, have been translated in several Countries out of Latin into their own native tongues.

Now the general verdict (after trial made) that hath passed, touching those formerly extant, is this, that, they are indeed of singular use and very advantageous to those of more discretion, (especially to such, as have already got a smattering in Latin) to help their memories to retain what they have scatteringly gotten here and there, and to furnish them with many words, which (perhaps) they had not formerly read, or so well observed; but to young Children *(whom we have chiefly to instruct) as those that are ignorant altogether of most things, and words,* they prove rather a more toyl and burden, than a delight, and furtherance.

For to pack up many words in memory, of things not conceived in the mind, is to fill the head with empty imaginations, and to make the learner more to admire their multitude, and variety *(and thereby to become discouraged;)* then to care to treasure them up, *in hopes to gain more knowledge of what they mean.*

He hath therefore in some of his later works seemed to move retrograde, and striven to come nearer to the reach of tender wits; and in this present Book, *he hath (according to my judgment,) descended to the very* Bottom *of what is to be taught, and proceeded (as Nature it self doth) in an orderly way; first to exercise the Senses well, by presenting their objects to them, and then to fasten upon the Intellect by impressing the first notions of things upon it, and linking them one to another by a rational discourse. Whereas indeed, We generally missing this way, do teach children as we do Parrats, to speak they know not what, nay, which is worse, we, t*aking the Way of teaching little ones by Grammar

mar only at the first, do pusle their imaginations with abstractive terms and secundary intentions, which, till they be somewhat acquainted with things, and the words belonging to them, in the language which they learn they cannot apprehend what they mean. *And this I guess to be the reason, why many greater persons do resolve sometimes, not to put a Child to School, till he be at lest eleven, or twelve years of age, presuming that he having then taken notice of most things, will sooner get the knowledge of the words which are applyed to them in any language. But the gross misdemeanour of such children for the most part, have taught many parents to be hasty enough to send their own to School, if not that they may learn, yet (at lest) that they may be kept out of harms way; and yet if they do not profit, for the time they have been at School, (no respect at all, being had of their years,) the Master shall be sure enough to bear the blame.*

So that a School-master had need to bend his wits to come within the compass of a Childes *capacity of six or seven years of age (seeing we have now such commonly brought to our Grammar-*Schooles *to learn the Latin Tongue) and to make that they may learn with as much delight and willingness, as himself would teach with dexterity, and ease. And at present I know no better Help to forward his young* Scholars *than this little* Book, *which was for this purpose contrived by the Author in the* German *and Latin Tongues.*

What profitable use may be made thereof respecting chiefly that his own Country and Language, he himself hath told you in his Preface; but what use we may here make of it in our Grammar Schooles, *as it is now translated into English, I shall partly declare: leaving all other men (according to my wont) to their own discretion, and liberty, to use it, or refuse it as they please. So soon then as a Child can read English perfectly and is brought us to School to learn Latine, I would have him together with his Accidence to be provided of this Book, in which he may at least once a day (besides his Accidence) be thus exercised*

I. *Let him* look over the Pictures with their general Titles *or Inscriptions, till he be able to turn readily to any one of them, and to tell its name either in English or Latin. By this means he shall have the Method of the* Book *in his head; and be easily furnished with the knowledge of most things; and instructed how to call them, when at any time he meeteth with them elswhere in their real forms.*

II. *Let*

II. *Let him* read the Description at large, *first in English, and afterwards in Latin, till he can readily read, and distinctly pronounce the words in both Languages, ever minding how they are spelled. And withall, let him take notice of the Figures inserted, and to what part of the Picture they direct by their like, till he be well able to find out every particular thing of himself, and to name it on a suddain, either in English, or Latine. Thus he shall not only gain the most primitive words, but be understandingly grounded in* Orthography, *which is a thing* too generally neglected *by us; partly because our English-Schools think that Children should learn it at the Latine, and our Latin-Schools suppose they have already learn'd it at the English; partly, because our Common Grammar is too much defective in this Part, and Scholars so little exercised therein, that they pass from Schools to the Universities, and return from thence (some of them) more unable to write true English, than either Latin or Greek. Not to speake of our ordinary Trades-men, many of whom write such false English, that none but themselves can interpret what they scribble, in their Bills, and shop Books.*

III. *Then let him* get the Titles and Descriptions by heart, *which he will more easily do by reason of those impressions which the viewing of the Pictures hath already made in his memory. And now let him also* learn, 1. To construe, *or give the words one by one, as they answer one another in Latin and English.* 2. To Parse, *according to the Rules (which I presume by this time) he hath learn'd in the first part of the Accidence; where I would have him,* tell what part of Speech any word is, and then what accidents belong to it; *but especially to* decline the Nouns, and conjugate the Verbs *according to the Examples in his Rudiments; and this doing will enable him to know the end and use of his Accidence. As for* the Rules of Genders of Nouns, and the præterperfect-tenses and Supines of Verbs, or those of concordance and Construction in the *latter part of the Accidence,* I would not have a Child much troubled with them, till *by the help of this Book* he can perfectly practise *so much of* Etimology, *as concerns the first Part of his Accidence only. For that, and this Book together being thorowly learn'd by at lest thrice going them over, will much prepare Children to go cheerfully forward in their Grammar, and School Authors, especially, if whil'st they are imployed herein they be taught also to write a fair, and legible hand.*

There is one thing to be given notice of, which I wish could have

have been remedied in this Tran.lation; that the Book *being writ in high-Dutch, doth express many things in reference to that Country and Speech which cannot without alteration of some Pictures, as well as words, be expressed in ours: for* the Symbolical Alphabet *is fitted for German Children rather than for ours.* And *whereas the words of that language go orderly one for one with the* Latine. *our English propriety of Speech will not admit the like. Therefore it will behoove those Masters, that intend to make use of this* Book, *to construe it* verbatim *to their young Scholars, who will quickly learn to do it of themselves, after they be once acquainted with the first words of Nouns, and* Verbs *and their manner of variation.*

Such a work as this, *I observe to have been formerly much* desired *by some experienced* Teachers *and I my self had some years since (whil'st my own* Child *lived) begun the like (having found it most agreeable to the best witted* Children, *who* are most taken up with Pictures from their Infancy because by them the knowledge of things which they seem to represent (*and whereof Children are as yet ignorant*) are most easily conveyed to their Understanding.) *but for as much as the work is now done (though in some things not so completely, as it were to be wished) I rejoyce in the use of it, and desist in my own undertakings for the present. And because* any good thing is the better, being the more communicated: *I have herein imitated a Child who is forward to impart to others what himself hath well liked. You then that have the care of little Children, do not too much trouble their thoughts and clog their memories with bare Grammar Rudiments, which to them are harsh in getting, and fluid in retaining; (because indeed to them they signifie nothing, but a meer swimming notion of a general term, which they know not what it meaneth till they comprehend also particulars but by this or the like Subsidiarie, inform them, first with some knowledge of things, and words wherewith to express them, and then their Rules of speaking will be better understood and more firmly kept in mind. Else how should a* Child *conceive what a Rule meaneth when he neither knoweth what the* Latine *word importeth, nor what manner of thing it is which is signified to him in his own native Language which is given him thereby to understand the Rule? For Rules consisting of generalities are delivered (as I may say) at a third hand, presuming first the things and then the words to be already apprehended touching which they are made*

I

I might indeed enlarge upon this Subject, it being the very Basis of our Profession, to search into the way of Childrens taking hold by little and little of what we teach them, *that so we may apply our selves to their reach, but I leave the observation hereof to your own daily exercise, and experience got thereby.*

And I pray God the fountain and giver of all wisdom, that hath bestowed upon u this gift of Teaching, so to inspire and direct us by his grace, that we may train up Children in his Fear, and in the knowledge of his Son Jesus Christ our Lord; and then no doubt our teaching and their learning of other things subordinate to these, will by the assistance of his blessed Spirit make them able and willing to do him faithful Service both in Church and Common-wealth as long as they live here, that so they may be eternally blessed with him hereafter. This I beseech you, beg for me and mine, as I shall daily do for you and yours, at the Throne of Gods heavenly grace, and remain while I live

Ready to serve you, as I truly love and honour you, and labour willingly in the same Profession with you,

CHARLES HOOLE.

From my School, in *Lothbury*, London, *Jan.* 25. 1658.

N. B. Those Heads or Descriptions which concern things beyond the present apprehension of Childrens wits, as, those of Geography, Astronomy, or the like, I would have omitted, till the rest be learned, and a Child be *better able to understand them.*

The

The Judgement of Mr. Hezekiah Woodward, *sometimes an* eminent Schoolmaster in LONDON, *touching a work of this Nature; in his* Gate to Sciences, *Chap.* 2.

CErtainly *the use of Images, or Representations is great:* If we could make our words as legible to Children as pictures are, their information there-from would be quickened and surer. But so we cannot do, though we must do what we can. *And if we had Books, wherein are the Pictures of all Creatures, Herbs, Beasts, Fish, Fowles, they would stand us in great stead.* For *Pictures are the most intelligible Books, that Children can look upon. They come closest to nature*; nay, *saith* Scaliger, *Art exceeds her.*

Orbis,

ORBIS SENSUALIUM PICTUS.

A WORLD Of *THINGS* Obvious to the SENSES Drawn in PICTURES.

I.

Invitation. *Invitatio.*

The Master and the Boy.

M. Come Boy, learn to be wise.

P. What doth this mean, to be wise?

M. To understand rightly, to do rightly, and to speak out rightly, all that are necessary.

P. Who will teach me this?

M. I, by Gods help.

P. How?

Magister & Puer.

M. Veni, Puer! disce sapere.

P. Quid hoc est, *Sapere*?

M. Omnia, quæ *necessaria*, rectè *intelligere*, rectè *agere*, rectè *eloqui*.

P. Quis me hoc docebit?

M. Ego, cum DEO.

P. Quomodo?

M. I will guide thee thorow all,
I will ſhew thee all.
I will name thee all.

M. Ducam te, per omnia,
Oſtendam tibi omnia.
Nominabo tibi omnia.

P. See, here I am; lead me in the name of God.

P. En adſum; duc me, in nomine DEI.

M. Before all things, thou oughteſt to learn the plain *ſounds*, of which mans ſpeech conſiſteth; which living Creatures know how to make, and thy tongue knoweth how to imitate, and thy hand can picture out.

M. Ante omnia, debes diſcere ſimplices *Sonos*, ex quibus conſtat *Sermo* humanus; quos, *Animalia* ſciunt *formare*, & tua *Lingua* ſcit *imitari*, & tua *Manus* poteſt *pingere*.

Afterwards we will go into the world, and we will view all things.

Poſtea ibimus in *Mundum*, & ſpectabimus omnia.

Here thou haſt a lively and vocal Alphabet.

Alphabetum vivum & vocale habes hîc.

Cornix cornicatur. *á á* A a
The Crow cryeth.

Agnus balat. *be e e* B b
The Lamb blaiteth.

Cicáda ſtridet. *ci ci* C c
The Graſhopper chirpeth.

Upupa dicit. *du du* D d
The Whooppoo ſaith.

Infans éjulat. *é é é* E e
The Infant cryeth.

Ventus flat. *fi fi* F f
The wind bloweth.

Anſer gingrit. *ga ga* G g
The Gooſe gaggleth.

Os halat. *háh háh* H h
The Mouth breatheth out.

Mus mintrit. *i i i* I i
The Mouſe chirpeth.

Anas tetrinnit. *kha kha* K k
The Duck quacketh.

Lupus ululat. *lu ulu* L l
The Woolf howleth.

Urſus murmurat. *mum mum* M m
The Bear grumbleth.

Felis clamat. *nau nau* N n
The Cat cryeth.

Auriga clamat. *ó ó ó* O o
The Carter cryeth.

Pullus pipit. *pi pi* P p
The Chicken peepeth.

Cúculus cúculat. *kuk ku* Q q
The Cuckow singeth cuckow.

Canis ríngitur. *err* R r
The Dog grinneth.

Serpens ſibilat. *ſi* S s
The Serpent hiſſeth.

Graculus clamat. *tac tac* T t
The Jay cryeth.

Bubo ululat. *u u* U u
The Owl hooteth.

Lepus vagit. *va* W w
The Hare squeaketh.

Rana coaxat. *coax* X x
The Frog croketh.

Aſinus rudit. *y y y* Y y
The Aſſe brayeth.

Tabanus dicit. *ds ds* Z z
The Breeze or Horſe-flie ſaith.

II.

God — *Deus.*

2

GOD is of himself, from everlasting to everlasting,	*DEUS* est ex seipso, ab æterno in æternum,
A most perfect and a most blessed Being.	*Ens* perfectissimum & beatissimum.
In his Essence Spiritual and one.	*Essentiâ* Spiritualis, & Unus.
In his Personality, Three.	*Hypostasi,* Trinus.
In his Will.	*Voluntate.*

Holy

Holy,	Sanctus,
Just,	Justus,
Merciful,	Clemens,
and true.	verax,
In his Power,	*Potentiâ*,
very great:	Maximus.
In his Goodness,	*Bonitate*,
very good.	Optimus.
In his Wisdome,	*Sapientiâ*,
unmeasurable.	immensus:
A Light	*Lux*
inaccessible;	inaccessa;
and yet all	& tamen
in all:	Omnia in omnibus;
Every where,	Ubique,
and no where:	& nullibi:
The chiefest Good,	Summum *bonum*.
and the only unexhausted fountain of all good things:	& bonorum omnium Fons solus, & inexhaustus.
As the Creator,	Omnium Rerum
so the Governor,	quas vocamus
and Preserver of all	*Mundum*,
things, which	ut *Creator*,
we call the	ita *Gubernator*
World.	& *Conservator*.

III.

Mundus.

3

The World.

The

The Heaven 1.	*Cœlum* 1.
hath fire,	habet *Ignem*,
and Stars.	& *Stellas*.
The Clouds 2.	*Nubes* 2.
hang	pendent
in the air.	in *Aere*.
Birds 3.	*Aves* 3.
flie	volant
under the Clouds.	ſub Nubibus.
Fiſhes 4.	*Piſces* 4.
ſwim	natant
in the water.	in *Aquâ*.
The Earth	*Terra*
hath Hills 5	habet *Montes*, 5.
Woods 6.	*Sylvas*, 6.
Fields 7.	*Campos*, 7.
Beaſts 8.	*Animalia*, 8.
And Men 9.	*Homines*, 9.
Thus,	Ita,
the greateſt	ſunt plena
bodies	Habitatoribus ſuis,
of the World,	quatuor *Elementa*,
the four Elements,	Mundi
are full of their own	maxima
Inhabitants.	Corpora.

IV. *Cœ-*

IV.

Cœlum.

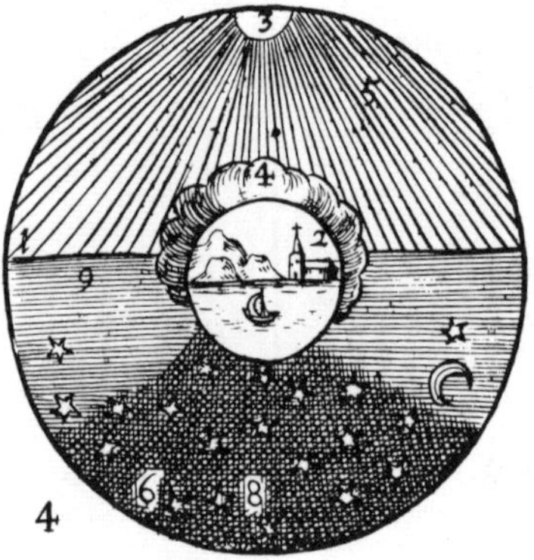

The Heaven.

The

The Heaven 1.	*Cœlum* 1.
is wheeled about,	rotatur,
and encompasseth	& ambit
the Earth 2.	*Terram* 2.
standing in	ſtantem in medio.
the middle.	
The Sun 3.	*Sol* 3.
wheresoever it is	ubi ubi eſt,
shineth perpetually,	fulget perpetuò,
howsoever dark	ut ut
Clouds 4.	*Nubila* 4.
may take it from us;	eum à nobis eripiant;
and by its rayes 5.	facítque ſuis *Radiis* 5.
it causeth light,	*Lucem*;
and the light, Day.	Lux *Diem*.
On the other side	Ex oppoſito,
over against it is	ſunt *Tenebræ* 6.
Darkneſs 6.	inde *Nox*.
and thence Night.	
In the Night,	Nocte,
shineth the Moon 7.	ſplendet *Luna*, 7.
and the Stars 8.	& *Stellæ* 8.
glister, and twinckle.	micant, ſcintillant.
In the Evening 9.	Veſperi 9.
is Twilight,	eſt *Crepuſculum*:
In the Morning, 10.	Mane *Aurora* 10.
the breaking, and	& *Diluculum*.
dawning of the Day.	

V. Fire

V.

Fire. Ignis.

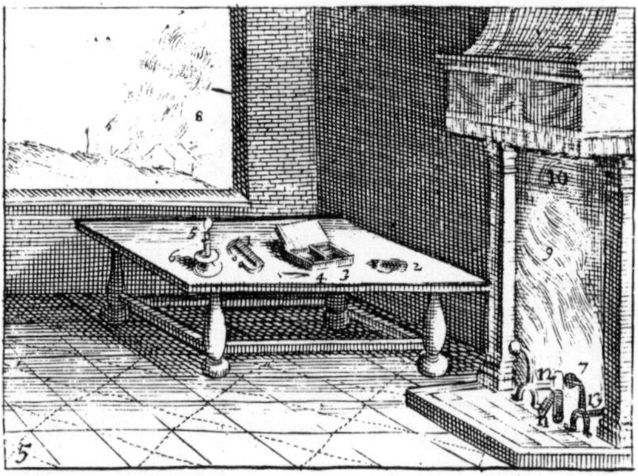

The Fire	*Ignis*
gloweth, burneth, and	ardet, urit,
consumeth to ashes.	cremat.
A spark of it struck	Ejus *Scintilla*,
out of a Flint	ope *Chalybis* 1.
(or Fierstone) 2.	è *Silice* (*Pyrite*) 2.
by means of a Steel 1.	elisa,
and taken by tinder in	& in *Suscitabulo* 3.
a tinder-box 3.	à *Fomite* excepta,
lighteth a match 4.	*Sulphuratum* 4.
and after that	
a Candle 5,	& inde *Candelam* 5.
or a Stick, 6.	vel *Lignum* 6.
and causeth	accendit,
a flame 7.	& *Flammam* 7. excitat

or

or blaze, 8.
which
catcheth hold
of the houses.
Smoak, 9.
ascendeth there-from
which,
sticking to the
Chimney 10.
turneth into soot.

Of a Fire-brand,
(or burning stick,)
is made a
Brand 11.
(or quenched
stick)
Of a hot Coal
(red-hot piece
of a fire-brand)
is made a Coal 12.
(or a dead
sinder.)
That,
which remaineth,
is at last
Ashes 13.
and Embers
(or hot Ashes.)

vel *Incendium* 8.
quod
ædificia
corripit.
Fumus 9.
inde ascendit,
qui,
adhærens
Camino, 10.
abit in *Fuliginem*.

Ex *Torre*,
(ligno
ardente,)
fit *Titio* 11.
(lignum
extinctum)
Ex *Prunâ*,
(candente
torris particulâ)
fit *Carbo* 12.
(*particula
mortua*.)
Tandem,
quod
remanet,
est *Cinis* 13.
& *Favilla*
(cinis ardens.)

VI. *Aër*.

VI.

Aer.

The Air.

A cool Air 1.	*Aura* 1.
breatheth gently.	spirat leniter.
The Wind 2.	*Ventus* 2.
bloweth strongly.	flat validè.
A Storm 3.	*Procella* 3.
throweth down Trees.	sternit Arbores.
A Whirl-wind 4.	*Turbo* 4.
turneth it self in a round compass.	se agit in gyrum.
A wind under ground 5.	Ventus *subterraneus* 5.
causeth an Earthquake.	excitat *Terræ-motum*;
An Earthquake, causeth gapings of the Earth, (and falls of Houses.) 6.	Terræ-motus facit *Labes* (ruinas.) 6.

VII.

Aqua.

The Water.

The

The water	*Aqua*
ſpringeth	ſcatet
out of a fountain, 1.	e *Fonte*, 1.
floweth downwards in	defluit
a brook, 2.	in *Torrente*, 2.
runneth	manat
in a beck, 3.	in *Rivo*, 3.
ſtandeth	ſtat
in a pond, 4.	in *Stagno*, 4.
glideth	fluit
in the ſtream, 5.	in *Flumine*, 5.
is whirled about in a	gyratur
whirl-pit 6.	in *Vortice*, 6.
and cauſeth	facit
Fens. 7.	*Paludes*. 7.
The River	Flumen
hath	habet
Banks. 8.	*Ripas*. 8.
The Sea	*Mare*
maketh	facit
Shores, 9.	*Littora*, 9.
Bayes, 10.	*Sinus*, 10.
Capes, 11.	*Promontoria*, 11.
Iſlands, 12.	*Inſulas*, 12.
Almoſt Iſlands, 13.	*Peninſulas*, 13.
Necks of Land, 14.	*Iſthmos*, 14.
Straights, 15.	*Freta*, 15.
and hath in it	& habet
Rocks. 16.	*Scopulos*. 16.

VIII.

The Clouds. *Nubes.*

A vapour 1.
aſcendeth from the
water.
From it
a Cloud 2.
is made, and
a white Miſt. 3.
near tne
Earth.
Rain 4.
and a ſmall ſhower
diſtilleth out of a
Cloud,
drop by drop.

Ex *aquâ*
aſcendit
Vapor. 1.
Inde fit
Nubes 2.
& propè terram
Nebula. 3.
E *Nube*
guttatim ſtillat
Pluvia 4.
& *Imber.*

Which	Quæ,
being frozen,	gelata,
is Hail ; 5.	*Grando* ; 5.
half-frozen,	semigelata,
is Snow ; 6.	*Nix* ; 6.
being warm	calefacta,
is Mel-dew.	*Rubigo* est.
In a Rainy Cloud,	In nube pluviosâ,
set over against the Sun, the Rain-bow 7.	Soli oppositâ,
appeareth.	apparet *Iris*. 7.
A drop	*Gutta*,
falling into the	incidens in aquam,
water, maketh	facit
a Bubble ; 8.	*Bullam* ; 8.
many Bubbles	multæ Bullæ
make	faciunt
froth. 9.	*Spumam*. 9.
Frozen water	Aqua congelata
is called Ice, 10.	*Glacies*, 10.
Dew congealed,	*Ros* congelatus,
a white Frost.	*Pruina*, dicitur.
Thunder	Ex
is made of a brimstone-like vapour,	vapore sulphureo fit *Tonitru*,
which,	quod,
breaking out of a cloud	erumpens è nube
with lightning, 11.	cum *Fulgure*, 11.
thundereth and striketh	tonat
with lightening.	& fulminat.

IX.

Terra.

The Earth.

It

In the Earth	In *Terrâ*
are	ſunt
high Mountains 1.	*Montes* 1, alti,
Deep Valleys, 2.	*Valles* 2. profundæ,
Hills Riſing, 3.	*Colles* 3. elevati,
Hollow Caves, 4.	*Speluncæ* 4. cavæ,
Plain Fields, 5.	*Campi* 5. plani,
Shady Woods. 6.	*Sylvæ* 6. opacæ.

X.

Terræ-Fœtûs.

10

The Fruits of the Earth.

The

A meadow 1.	*Pratum* 1.
yieldeth	fert
Grass,	*Gramina*,
with Flowers	cum *Floribus*
and Herbs,	& *Herbis*,
which being	quæ
cut down,	desecta,
are made Hay 2.	fiunt *Fœnum* 2.
A Field 3.	*Arvum* 3.
yieldeth Corn,	fert *Fruges*
and Pot-herbs 4.	& *Olera* 4.
	In *Sylvis* proveniunt
Mushroms, 5.	*Fungi*, 5.
Straw-berries, 6.	*Fraga*, 6.
Myrtle-trees, *&c.*	*Myrtilli*, &c.
Come up in	Sub Terrâ
woods.	nascuntur
Metals,	*Metalla*,
Stones,	*Lapides*,
and Minerals	*Mineralia*.
grow under the	
Earth.	

XI.

Metalla.

Metals.

Lead

Lead 1.	*Plumbum* 1.
is soft, and heavy.	est molle & grave.
Iron 2.	*Ferrum* 2.
is hard,	est durum,
and Steel 3.	& durior
harder.	*Calybs*. 3.
They make	E *Stanno*,
Tankards	faciunt
(or Cans) 4.	*Cantharos*; 4.
of Tin;	e *Cupro*,
Kettles 5.	*Ahena*, 5.
of Copper;	ex *Orichalco*,
Candlesticks 6.	*Candelabra*, 6.
of Lattin;	ex *Argento*;
Dollers 7.	*Thaleros*, 7.
of Silver;	ex *Auro*,
Ducates	*Scutatos*,
and Crown	(Ducatos)
pieces 8	& *Coronatos*. 8.
of Gold;	
Quick-silver,	*Argentum vivum*,
is alwaies liquid,	semper liquet,
and eateth thorow	& metalla
Metals.	corrodit.

XII.

Stones. — *Lapides.*

12

Sand 1.
and Gravel 2.
is Stone broken
into bits.
A great Stone 3.
is a piece of
a Rock (or Crag) 4.
A whet-stone 5.
A Flint, 6.

Arena 1.
& *Sabulum* 2.
est comminutus
Lapis.
Saxum 3.
est pars
Petræ (Cautis) 4.
Cos, 5.
Silex, 6.

Marmor

A Marble 7. &c.
are ordinary
stones.
A Load-stone 8.
draweth Iron to it.
Jewels 9.
are clear stones, as,

The Diamond white,
The Rubie red,
The Sapphire blew,
The Emerald green,
The Jacinth yellow,
&c. And they glitter being cut in fashion of the nails of ones hand.
Pearls,
and Unions 10.
grow in Shell-Fish,

Corals, 11.
in a Sea-shrub.
Amber, 12.
is gathered from the Sea.
Glass, 13.
is like Chrystal.

Marmor, 7. &c.
sunt lapides obscuri.

Magnes 8.
adtrahit ferrum.
Gemmæ 9.
sunt lapilli pellucidi, ut:
Adamas candidus,
Rubinus rubeus,
Sapphirus cæruleus,
Smaragdus viridis,
Hyacinthus luteus, &c.
& micant
ungulati.

Margaritæ
& *Uniones* 10.
crescunt
in conchis;
Corallia 11.
in Marinâ arbuscula.
Succinum 12.
colligitur
è mari.
Vitrum 13.
simile est
Crystallo.

XIII.

Tree. *Arbor.*

13

A Plant 1. groweth from a Seed.	E *Semine* procrescit *Planta*, 1.
A Plant waxeth to a Shoot, 2.	Planta abit in *Fruticem*, 2.
A Shoot, to a Tree, 3.	Frutex in *Arborem*, 3.
The Root 4. beareth up the Tree.	Arborem sustentat *Radix*. 4.

E Ra-

The Body or Stem 5.
riseth from the
Root.
The Stem
divideth it self
into Boughs 6.
and green branches 7.
made of
leaves 8.
The top 9.
is in the height.
The Stock 10.
is close to the roots.
A Log 11.
is the body feld down,
without boughs,
having
Bark
and Rinde 12.
Bait and
Heart 13.
Bird-lime 14.
groweth upon the
boughs, which also
sweat
Gumm,
Rosin,
Pitch, &c.

E Radice
surgit
Stirps (*Stemma*.) 5.
Stirps
se dividit
in *Ramos* 6.
& *Frondes*, 7.
factas
ex *Foliis* 8.
Cacumen 9.
in summo est.
Truncus 10.
adhæret radicibus.
Caudex 11.
est dejectus Stipes,
sine ramis:
habens
Corticem
& *Librum*, 12.
pulpam
& *medullam*, 13.
Viscum 14.
ramis adnascitur:
qui etiam
Gummi,
Resinam,
Picem, &c.
sudant.

Fructus

XIV.

Fruits of Trees. *Fructus Arborum.*

Fruits that have no shels are pulled from fruit-bearing trees.	*Poma* ab arboribus fructiferis decerpuntur.
The Apple 1. is round.	*Malum* 1. est rotundum.
The Pear 2. and Fig 3. are somewhat long.	*Pyrum* 2. & *Ficus* 3. sunt oblonga.
The Cherry 4. hangeth by a long start.	*Cerasum* 4. pendet longo *Pediolo*.
The Plumb 5. and Peach 6.	*Prunum* 5. & *Persicum* 6.

by

by a shorter.	breviori.
The Mulberry 7.	*Morum* 7.
by a very short one.	brevissimo.
The Wall-nut 8.	*Nux juglans* 8.
the Hasel-nut 9.	*Avellana* 9.
and Chest-nut 10.	& *Castanea* 10.
are wrapt in a	involuta sunt
Husk	*Cortici*
and a Shell.	& *Putamini.*
Barren trees	Steriles arbores
are 11.	sunt 11.
The Firr,	*Abies,*
the Elder,	*Alnus,*
the Birch,	*Betula,*
the Cypriss,	*Cupressus,*
the Beech,	*Fagus,*
the Ash,	*Fraxinus,*
the Sallow,	*Salix,*
the Linden-tree, *&c.*	*Tilia,* &c.
But the most of them	sed pleræque
affording shade.	umbriferæ.
But the Juniper 12.	At *Juniperus* 12.
and Bay-tree 13.	& *Laurus* 13.
yield	ferunt
Berries.	*Baccas,*
The Pine 14.	*Pinus* 14.
Pine-Apples.	*Strobilos.*
The Oak 15.	*Quercus* 15.
Acorns	*Glandes*
and Galls.	& *Gallas.*

XV.

Flowers. *Flores.*

The most noted amongst the Flowers,	Inter flores, notissimi,
In the beginning of the Spring, are the	Primo vere,
Violet 1.	*Viola* 1.
the Crow toes 2.	*Hyacinthus* 2.
the Daffadil 3.	*Narcissus* 3.
Then the Lillies, white and yellow 4.	Tum *Lilia*, *alba* & *lutea* 4.
and blew 5.	& *cœrulea* 5.
and the	Tardem
Rose 6.	*Rosa* 6.
and Clove-gillow-flower. 7. *&c.*	& *Caryophyllum*, 7. &c.

Of these	Ex his vientur
Garlands 8.	*Serta* 8.
and Nose-gays 9.	& *Servia* 9.
are tyed round with twigs.	
There are also sweet herbs added 10.	Adduntur etiam *Herbæ odoratæ* 10.
as, Marjoram,	ut, *Amaracus*,
Flower-gentle,	*Amaranthus*,
Rue,	*Ruta*,
Lavender,	*Lavendula*,
Rosemary,	*Rosmarinus* (Libanotis)
Hysop,	*Hyssopus*,
Spike,	*Nardus*,
Basil,	*Ocymum*,
Sage,	*Salvia*,
Mints, *&c.*	*Menta*, &c.
Amongst Field-flowers 11.	Inter Campestres, 11.
the most noted are,	notissimi sunt, Flores :
the May-lillie,	*Lilium convallium*,
Germander,	*Chamædrys*,
the Blew-bottle,	*Cyanus*,
Chamomel, &c.	*Chamæmelum*, &c.
And amongst herbs,	& Herbæ :
Trefoil,	*Cytisus* (Trifolium)
Wormwood,	*Absinthium*,
Sorrel,	*Acetosa*,
the Nettle, &c.	*Urtica*, &c.
The Tulip 12.	*Tulipa* 12.
is the grace of flowers,	Florum decus est,
but affording no smell.	sed odoris expers.

XVI.

Olera.

Pot-Herbs.

Pot-

Pot-herbs	In Hortis
grow in	naſcuntur
Gardens,	Olera,
as, Lettice 1.	ut, *Lactuca* 1.
Colewort 2.	*Braſſica* 2.
Onions 3.	*Cepa* 3.
Garlike 4.	*Allium* 4.
Gourd 5.	*Cucurbita* 5.
The Parſnep 6.	*Siſer* 6.
The Turnep 7.	*Rapa* 7.
The Rhadiſh 8.	*Raphanus minor* 8.
Horſe-Rhadiſh 9.	*Raphanus major* 9.
Perſelie 10.	*Petroſelinum* 10.
Cucumbers 11.	*Cucumeres* 11.
and Pompions 12.	*Pepones* 12.

XVII.

Fruges.

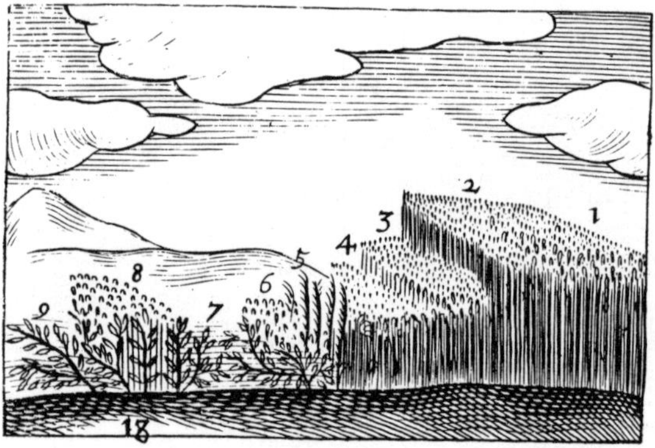

Corn.

Some Corn,	*Frumenta*,
grows upon a	quædam crescunt
Straw,	super *culmum*,
parted by knots,	distinctum *geniculis*,
as, Wheat, 1.	ut, *Triticum*, 1.
Rie, 2.	*Siligo*, 2.
Barley, 3.	*Hordeum* 3.
in which the Ear	in quibus *Spica*,
hath awnes, or else it is	habet Aristas,
without awnes, and it	aut est mutica,
nourisheth the Corns	fovetque *grana*
in the Husk.	in *glumâ*.
Some,	Quædam,
instead of an Ear,	pro Spicâ,
have a rizom	habent *Paniculam*,
(or plume) containing	continentem grana
the Corns by bunches,	fasciatim,
as, Oats, 4.	ut, *Avena*, 4.
Millit, 5.	*Milium*, 5.
Turkey-wheat. 6.	*Frumentum Saraceni-* (*cum* 6.
Pulse	*Legumina*
have Cods,	habent *Siliquas*,
which enclose the	quæ grana
corns in two shales,	includunt *valvulis*,
as, Pease, 7.	ut, *Pisum*, 7.
Beans, 8.	*Faba*, 8.
Vetches, 9.	*Vicia*, 9.
and those that are less	&, his minora,
than these, Lentils and	*Lentes*
Urles (or Tares.)	& *Cicera*.

XVIII.

Frutices.

Shrubs.

A Plant	Planta,
being greater, and	major herba
harder than an Herb,	& durior,
is called a Shrub,	dicitur *Frutex*,
such as are :	ut sunt :
In Banks,	In ripis
and ponds,	& stagnis,
the Rush, 1.	*Juncus*, 1.
the Bul-rush, 2.	enodis *Scirpus*
or Cane without knots,	[Canna] 2.
bearing Cats tails,	ferens *Typhos*,
and the Reed 3.	& nodosa
which is knotty and	intusque cava
hollow within.	*Arundo* 3.
Elsewhere 4.	Alibi, 4.
the Rose,	*Rosa*,
the Bastard-Corinths,	*Ribes*,
the Elder,	*Sambucus*,
the Juniper.	*Juniperus*.
Also the Vine 5.	Item *Vitis*, 5.
which putteth	quæ emittit
forth branches 6.	*Palmites*, 6.
and these tendrels 7.	& hi *Capreolos*, 7.
Vine-leaves, 8.	*Pampinos*, 8.
and bunches	ac *Racemos*, 9.
of grapes 9.	quorum *Scapo*
on the stalk	pendent *Uvæ*,
whereof hang grapes,	continentes
which contein Grape-	Acinos.
stones.	

XIX.

Animalia, & Primùm Aves.

Living-Creatures, and first Birds.

A living Creature,	*Animal*,
liveth, perceiveth,	vivit, ſentit,
moveth it ſelf;	movet ſe;
is born, dieth;	naſcitur, moritur;
is nouriſhed,	nutritur,
and groweth; ſtandeth,	& creſcit; ſtat,
or ſitteth, or lyeth,	aut ſedet, aut cubat,
or goeth.	aut graditur.
A Bird, (Fiſher 1.	*Avis*,
(here the Kings	(hîc *Halcyon* 1.
making her neſt	in mari
in the Sea)	nidulans,)
is covered with	tegitur
Feathers 2.	*Plumis*, 2.
flyeth with Wings 3.	volat *Pennis*, 3.
hath two pinions 4.	habet duas *Alas*, 4.
and as many Feet 5.	totidem *Pedes*, 5.
A Tail, 6.	*Caudam*, 6.
and a Bill. 7.	& *Roſtrum*. 7.
The Shee, 8.	*Fœmella*, 8.
layeth Eggs, 10.	in *Nido*, 9.
in a Neſt, 9.	ponit *Ova*, 10.
and ſitting upon them,	iiſque incubans,
hatcheth	excludit
young ones. 11.	*Pullos*. 11.
An Egg is covered	*Ovum*
with a Shell, 12.	tegitur *Teſtâ*, 12.
under which is	ſub quâ eſt
the White, 14.	*Albumen*, 14.
in this the Yolk. 13.	in hoc *Vitellus*. 13.

XX.

Aves Domesticæ.

Tame Foul.

The

The Cock 1.	*Gallus* 1.
(which croweth in a morning)	(qui manè cantat)
hath a Comb, 2.	habet *Cristam*, 2.
and Spurs; 3.	& *Calcaria*; 3.
being gelded, he is	castratus,
called a Capon.	dicitur *Capo*,
and is crammed	& saginatur
in a Coop. 4.	in *Ornithotrophio*. 4.
A Hen, 5.	*Gallina*, 5.
scrapeth the Dunghill,	ruspatur *fimetum*,
and picketh up Corns:	& colligit grana:
as also the Pigeons, 6.	sicut & *Columbæ*, 6.
(which are brought up	(quæ educantur
in a Pigeon-house 7.)	in *Columbario*; 7.)
and the Turky-Cock 8.	& *Gallopavus*, 8.
with his Turky-Hen. 9.	cum suâ *Meleagride*. 9.
The gay Peacock, 10	Formosus *Pavo*, 10.
prideth in his feathers.	pennis superbit.
The Stork, 11.	*Ciconia*, 11.
buildeth her nest on the top of the House.	in tecto nidificat.
The Swallow, 12.	*Hirundo*, 12.
the Sparrow, 13.	*Passer*, 13.
the Mag pie, 14.	*Pica*, 14.
the Jackdaw, 15.	*Monedula*, 15.
and the Bat, 16.	& *Vespertilio*, 16.
(or Flittermouse)	(Mus alatus)
use to flie about	volitant circa
Houses.	Domus.

Oscines.

XXI.

Oscines.

Singing-Birds.

The Nightingal 1.	*Luscinia* (*Philomela*) 1.
singeth	cantat
the sweetliest of all.	suavissimè omnium.
The Lark 2.	*Alauda* 2.
singeth	cantillat,
as she flieth in the air;	volitans in aere;
The Quail, 3.	*Coturnix*, 3.
sitting on the ground;	humi sedens;
Others, (Trees 4.	Cæteræ,
on the boughs of	in ramis arborum, 4.
as, the Canary-bird,	ut, *Luteola* peregrina,
The Chaffinch,	*Fringilla*,
The Goldfinch,	*Carduelis*,
The Siskin,	*Acanthis*,
The Linnet,	*Linaria*,
The little Titmouse,	parvus *Parus*,
The Wood-wall,	*Galgulus*,
The Robin-red-breast,	*Rubecula*,
the hedge sparrow, &c.	*Curruca*, &c.
The party-coloured	
Parret 5.	*Psittacus* 5. discolor,
The Black-bird, 6.	*Merula*, 6.
The Stare, 7.	*Sturnus*, 7.
with the Mag-pie,	cum *Picâ*.
and the Jay,	& *Monedulâ*,
learn	discunt
to frame Mens	humanas voces
Words.	formare.
A great many	Pleræque,
are wont to be shut	solent includi
in Cages 8.	*Caveis*. 8.

XXII.

Aves Campestres & Sylvestres.

Birds that haunt the Fields and Woods.

The

The Ostrich 1.	*Struthio* 1.
is the greatest Bird.	est ales maximus.
The Wren 2.	*Regulus* 2.(Trochilus)'
is the least.	minimus.
The Owl 3.	*Noctua* 3.
the most despicable.	despicatissimus.
The Whoophoo 4.	*Upupa* 4.
the most nasty,	sordidissimus, (bus.
for it eateth dung.	vescitur enim stercori-
The Bird of Para-	*Manucodiata* 5.
dice 5. is very rare.	rarissimus.
The Pheasant 6.	*Phasianus* 6.
the Bustard 7.	*Tarda* (Otis) 7.
the deaf wild Peacock 8	*Tetrao* 8. surdus,
the Moor-Hen 9.	*Attagen* 9.
the Partridge 10.	*Perdix* 10.
the Wood-cock 11.	*Gallinago* (Rusticola) 11.
and the Thrush 12.	& *Turdus*, 12.
are accounted dainties.	in deliciis habentur.
Amongst the rest,	Inter reliquas,
the best are the watch-	potissimæ sunt :
ful Crane 13.	*Grus* 13. pervigil,
the mournful Turtle 14.	*Turtur* 14. gemens,
the Cuckow 15.	*Cuculus* 15.
the Stock-dove,	*Palumbes*,
the Speight,	*Picus*,
the Jay,	*Garrulus*,
the Crow, &c. 16.	*Cornix*, &c. 16.

XXIII.

Aves Rapaces.

Ravenous Birds.

The Eagle, 1.	*Aquila*, 1.
the King of Birds,	Rex avium,
looketh upon the Sun.	Solem intuetur.
The Vulture, 2.	*Vultur*, 2.
and the Raven, 3.	& *Corvus*, 3.
feed upon	pascuntur
Carrion.	*morticinis* [cadaveribus.]
The Kite 4.	*Milvus* 4.
pursueth	insectatur
Chickens.	pullos gallinaceos.
The Falcon, 5.	*Falco*, 5.
The Hobbie, 6.	*Nisus*, 6.
and the Hawk, 7.	& *Accipiter*, 7.
catch at little Birds.	captant aviculas.
The Gerfalcon, 8.	*Astur*, 8.
Pigeons,	columbas,
and greater Birds.	& aves majores.

XXIV.

Aves Aquaticæ.

Water Fowl.

The

The white Swan, 1.	*Olor* 1. candidus,
The Goose, 2.	*Anser*, 2.
and the Duck, 3.	& *Anas*, 3.
swim up and down.	natant.
The Cormorant 4.	*Mergus*, 4.
diveth.	se mergit.
Add to these	His adde
the water-hen,	*Fulicam*,
and the Pelecan, &c. 10.	*Pelecanum*, &c. 10.
The Osprey, 5.	*Haliaetus* 5.
and the Sea-mew, 6.	& *Gavia*, 6.
flying down-wards	devolantes;
use to catch fish,	
but the Heron 7.	sed *Ardea* 7.
standing on the	stans in ripis,
Banks.	captant pisces.
The Bittern, 8.	*Butio*, 8.
putteth his Bill	rostrum aquæ inserit,
into the water,	& ut bos mugit.
and belloweth like	
an Ox.	
The Water-wagtail 9.	*Motacilla* 9.
waggeth the tail.	motat caudam.

XXV.

Insecta volantia.

Flying-vermin.

The Bee 1.	*Apis* 1.
maketh Honey,	facit Mel,
which the	quod depascit
Drone 2. devoureth.	*Fucus.* 2.
The Wasp, 3.	*Vespa*, 3.
and the Hornet, 4.	& *Crabro*, 4.
molest with a sting;	aculeo infestant:
and the Gad-bee	& Pecus imprimis,
(or Breese) 5.	*Oestrum* (Asilus;) 5.
especially Cattel;	nos autem,
but the Flye 6.	*Musca* 6.
and the Gnat 7. us.	& *Culex.* 7.
The Cricket 8.	*Gryllus* 8.
singeth.	cantillat.
The Butterflie 9.	*Papilio* 9.
is a winged	est *Eruca* alata.
Caterpiller.	
The Beetle 10.	*Scarabæus* 10.
covereth her wings	tegit alas
with Cases.	Vaginis.
The Glow-worm 11.	*Cicindela* [Lampy-
shineth by night.	noctu nitet. (ris] 11.

XXVI.

Quadrupedia,
& Primùm Domeſtica.

Four-Footed-Beaſts,
and firſt thoſe about the Houſe.

The

The Dog 1.
with the Whelp 2.
is the keeper of
the House.

Canis 1.
cum *Catello*, 2.
est custos Domûs.

The Cat 3.
riddeth the House
of Mice; 4.
which also a
Mouse-trap, 5. doth.

Felis (Catus) 3.
domum purgat
à *Muribus*; 4.
quod etiam facit
Muscipula. 5.

The Squirrel, 6.
The Ape, 7.
and the Monkey, 8.
are kept at home
for delight.

Sciurus, 6.
Simia, 7.
& *Cercopithecus*, 8.
domi habentur
delectamento.

The Dormouse, 9.
and other
greater Mice, 10.
as, the Weesel,
The Martin,
and the Ferret,
trouble the House.

Glis, 9.
& cæteri
Mures majores, 10.
ut, *Mustela*,
Martes,
Viverra,
domum infestant.

XXVII.

Pecora.

Heard Cattel.

The

The Bull 1.	*Taurus* 1.
the Cow 2.	*Vacca* 2.
and the Calf 3.	& *Vitulus* 3.
are covered with hair.	pilis teguntur.
The Ram, the Wea-	*Aries* (Vervex) 4.
the Ewe 5. (ther 4.	*Ovis* 5.
and the Lamb 6.	cum *Agno* 6.
bear wool.	Lanam gestant.
The Hee-goat, the gelt-Goat 7.	*Hircus* (Caper) 7.
with the Shee-goat 8.	cum *Caprâ* 8.
and Kid 9.	& *Hœdo* 9.
have	habent
shag-hair and beards.	*Villos & aruncos.*
The Hog, the Sow 10.	*Porcus* (Scrofa) 10.
and the Pigs 11.	cum *Porcellis* 11.
have bristles,	habent *Setas*;
but not horns;	at non *Cornua*,
but cloven feet too,	sed etiam
as those other	*Ungulas bisulcas*,
have.	ut illa.

Jumenta.

XXVIII.

Jumenta.

Labouring Beasts.

The

The Aſs 1. and the Mule 2. carry burdens.	*Aſinus* 1. & *Mulus* 2. geſtant Onera.
The Horſe 3. (which a Main 4. graceth) carrieth us.	*Equus* 3. (quem ornat *Juba* 4.) nos ipſos.
The Camel 5. carrieth the Merchant with his Wares.	*Camelus* 5. mercatorem cum mercibus ſuis.
The Elephant 6. draweth his meat to him with his Trunk. 7.	*Elephas* (Barus) 6. pabulum adtrahit *Proboſcide* 7.
He hath two Teeth 8. ſtanding out, and is able to carry full thirty men.	*Dentes* duos 8. habet prominentes, & portare poteſt etiam triginta Viros.

XXIX.

Feræ Pécudes.

Wild Cattel.

The

The Buff 1.	*Urus* 1.
and the Buffal 2.	& *Bubalus* 2.
are wild Bulls.	sunt feri boves.
The Elke 3.	*Alces*
being bigger than an	major equo,
horse (whose back	(cujus tergus
is impenetrable)	est impenetrabilis)
hath	habet
knaggy horns;	ramosa cornua;
as also the Hart 4.	ut & *Cervus* 4.
But the Roe 5.	Sed *Caprea* 5.
and the Hinde Calf al-	cum *Hinnulo*,
most none;	ferè nulla;
The Stone-back 6.	*Capricornus* 6.
huge great ones;	prægrandia;
The Wild-goat 7.	*Rupicapra* 7.
hath very little ones,	minuta,
by which she hangeth	quibus se
her self on a rock.	ad rupem suspendit;
The Unicorn 8.	*Monoceros* 8.
hath but one,	unum,
but that a precious one.	sed pretiosum.
The Boar 9.	*Aper* 9.
assaileth one with his tushes.	dentibus grassatur.
The Hare 10.	*Lepus* 10.
is fearful.	pavet.
The Cony 11.	*Cuniculus* 11.
diggeth the earth;	terram perfodit;
As also the Mole 12.	Ut & *Talpa* 12.
which maketh hillocks.	quæ grumos facit.

Fera

XXX.

Feræ Bestiæ.

Wild Beasts.

Wild

Wild Beasts	*Bestiæ*
have sharp paws,	habent acutos Ungues
and teeth, and are	& dentes, suntque
flesh-eaters.	carnivoræ.
As the Lyon 1.	Ut, *Leo*, 1.
the King of four-footed	Rex Quadrupedum,
beasts, having a main,	jubatus,
with the Lioness;	cum *Leænâ*;
The spotted	Maculosus
Panther 2.	*Pardus* Panthera) 2.
The Tygre 3.	*Tygris* 3.
the cruellest of all;	immanissima omnium;
The shaggy	Villosus
Bear 4.	*Ursus* 4.
The ravenous	Rapax
Wolf 5.	*Lupus* 5.
The quicksighted	*Lynx* 6.
Ounce 6.	visu pollens.
The tayled	Caudata
Fox 7.	*Vulpes* 7.
the craftiest of all.	omnium astutissima.
The Hedge-hog 8.	*Erinaceus* 8.
is prickly.	est aculeatus.
The Badger 9.	*Melis* 9.
delighteth in holes.	latebris gaudet.

Serpentes

XXXI.

Serpentes & Reptilia.

Serpents and creeping things.

Snakes creep by winding themſelves ;	*Angues*, repunt ſinuando ſe :
The Adder 1. in the wood ;	*Coluber* 1. in Silvâ ;
The Water-Snake 2. in the water ;	*Natrix* (hydra) 2. in Aquâ ;
The Viper 3. among great ſtones ;	*Vipera* 3. in Saxis ;
The Aſpe 4. in the fields ;	*Aſpis* 4. in Campis ;
The Boa (or Milk-Snake 5.) in Houſes.	*Boa* 5. in Domibus.
The Slow-worm 6. is blind.	*Cæcilia* 6. eſt cœca.
The Lizzard 7. and the Salamander 8. (that liveth long in the fire) have feet.	*Lacerta* 7. *Salamandra* 8. in igne vivax, Pedes habent.
The Dragon 9. a winged Serpent killeth with his breath ;	*Draco* 9. *Serpens alatus*, halitu ;
The Baſilisk 10. with his eyes,	*Baſiliſcus* 10. Oculis ;
and the Scorpion 11. with his poyſonous tayl.	*Scorpius* 11. venenatâ cauda, necantes.

XXXII.

Crawling Vermin. *Insecta repentia.*

Worms	*Vermes*,
gnaw things ;	res rodunt :
The Earth worm 1.	*Lumbricus* 1.
the Earth ;	terram ;
The Caterpillar 2.	*Eruca* 2.
the Plant ;	plantam ;
The Grashopper 3.	*Cicada* 3.
the Fruits ;	fruges ;
The Mite 4.	*Curculio* 4.
the Corn ;	frumenta ;

The Timber-worm 5.	*Teredo* (coſſus) 5.
Wood;	ligna;
The Moth 6.	*Tinea* 6.
a garment;	Veſtem;
The Book-worm 7.	*Blatta* 7.
a Book;	Librum;
Maggots 8.	*Termines* 8.
Fleſh and Cheeſe;	carnem & caſeum;
Hand-worms	*Acari*,
the hair.	Capillum.
The Skipping Flea 9.	Saltans *Pulex* 9.
the Lowſe 10.	*Pediculus* 10.
and the ſtinking	
Wall-louſe 11.	fœtens *Cimex* 11.
bite us.	nos mordent.
The Tike 12.	*Ricinus* 12.
is a blood-ſucker.	ſanguiſugus eſt.
The Silk-worm 13.	*Bombyx* 13.
maketh ſilk.	facit ſericum.
The Piſmire 14.	*Formica* 14.
is painful.	eſt laborioſa.
The Spider 15.	*Aranea* 15.
weaveth a Cobweb,	texit araneum,
nets for flies.	muſcis retia.
The Snail 16.	*Cochlea* 16.
carrieth about her	teſtam circumfert.
Snail-horn.	

XXXIII.

Amphibia.

Creatures that live as well by Water as by Land.

Creatures that
live by land and by
water are,

The Crocodile 1.
a cruel
and preying Beast
of the River Nilus;

The Castor or Beaver 2.
having
feet like a Gooses
to swim,
and a scaly tail;

The Otter 3.
the croaking Frog 4.
with the Toad,

The Tortoise 5.
covered above
and beneath
with shels,
as with a Target.

In terra & aqua
viventia sunt,

Crocodilus 1.
immanis
& prædatrix bestia
Nili fluminis;

Castor (Fiber) 2.
habens
pedes anserinos
ad natandum,
& caudam squameam;

Lutra 3.
& coaxans *Rana* 4.
cum *Bufone*,

Testudo 5.
supra & infra
testis,
ceu scuto,
operta.

XXXIV.

River Fiſh and Pond Fiſh.	***Piſces Fluviatiles & Lacuſtres.***

A Fiſh	*Piſcis*
hath Fins 1.	habet *Pinnas* 1.
with which it ſwimeth,	quibus natat ;
and Gills 2. (breath,	& *Branchias*, 2.
by which it taketh	quibus reſpirat ;
and Prickles	& *Spinas*,
inſtead of bones :	loco oſſium :
beſides,	præterea,
the Male hath a Milt,	Mas, *lactes* ;
and the Female a Rone.	Fœmina, *Ova*.
Some	Quidam
have Scales,	habent *Squamas*,

as

as the Carp 3.
and the Luce or Pike 4.
Some are flick,
as the Eele 5.
and the Lamprey 6.
The Sturgion 7.
having a sharp snout,
groweth longer than
a man;
The Sheath-fish 8.
having wide cheeks,
is bigger then he.
But the Huson 9.
is the greatest.
Minewes 10.
swimming by shoals,
are the least.
Others of this sort,
are the Perch,
the Bley,
the Barbel,
the Esch, the Trout,
the Gudgeon, and
Trench 11.
The Crab-fish 12.
is covered with a shell,
and it hath claws,
and crawleth
forwards & backwards.
The Horse-leech 13.
sucketh blood.

ut *Carpio* 3.
Lucius (Lupus) 4.
Alii sunt glabri,
ut, *Anguilla* 5.
Mustela 6.
Accipenser (Sturio) 7.
mucronatus,
ultra longitudinem viri
excrescit;
Silurus 8.
bucculentus,
major illo est;
Sed maximus
Antaceus (Huso;) 9.
Apuæ 10.
gregatim natantes,
sunt minutissimi.
Alii hujus generis
sunt, *Perca*,
Alburnus,
Mullus (barbus)
Thymallus, *Trutta*,
Gobius,
Tinca, 11.
Cancer 12.
tegitur *crustâ*,
habetque *chelas*,
& graditur
porrò & retrò.
Hirudo 13.
sugit sanguinem.

XXXV.

Marini Pisces, & Conchæ.

Sea-Fish, and Shell-Fish.

The Whale 1.
is the greatest of
the Sea-fish.
  The Dolphin 2.
the swiftest;
  The Scate 3.
the most monstrous,
    Others are
the Lamprel, 4.
The Salmon, and the
lax, 5.
    There are also
Fish that flie. 6.
    Add
Herrings, 7.
which are brought
pickled, and Place, 8.
and Cods, 9.
which are brought dry,

and the Sea-monsters,
the Seal, 10.
and the Sea-horse, &c.
  Shel-fish 11.
have shels.
  The Oyster 12.
affordeth sweet meat.
  The Purple-fish 13.
purple;
  The other
Pearls, 14.

Piscium marinorum
maximus est
Balæna (Cetus) 1.
  Delphinus 2.
velocissimus;
  Raia 3.
monstrosissimus.
  Alii sunt,
Murænula, 4.
Salmo (Esox) 5.

  Dantur etiam
Volatiles. 6.
  Adde
Haleces, 7.
qui salsi,
& *Passeres*, 8.
cum *Asellis*, 9.
qui arefacti,
adferuntur :
& monstra marina,
Phocam, 10.
Hippopotamum, &c.
  Concha 11.
habet testas.
  Ostrea 12.
dat sapidam carnem.
  Murex 13.
purpuram;
  Alia, 14.
Margaritas.

Homo

XXXVI.

Homo.

Man.

Adam,

Adam, 1.
the firſt Man,
was made by God,
after the Image
of God, the ſixth day
of the Creation,
of a lump of Earth;
And Eve, 2.
the firſt Woman,
was made
of a Rib of the Man.
These, being tempted
by the Devil,
under the ſhape of
a Serpent, 3.
when they had eaten
of the fruit of the
forbidden Tree, 4.
were condemned
to miſery 5.
and death,
with all their
poſterity,
and caſt out of
Paradiſe 6.

Adamus, 1.
primus Homo,
ſextâ die
Creationis,
à Deo,
ad imaginem **Dei**,
è glebâ terræ;
Et *Heva*, 2.
prima Mulier,
e coſtâ viri,
formati ſunt.
Hi, à *Diabolo*,
ſub ſpecie
Serpentis, 3.
ſeducti, cum comede-
rent de fructu
arboris vetitæ, 4.
ad *miſeriam* 5.
& mortem,
cum omni
poſteritate ſuâ,
damnati
& è *Paradiſo* 6.
ejecti ſunt.

XXXVII.

Septem Ætates Hominis.

The Seven Ages of Man.

A Man is	Homo eſt
firſt an Infant, 1.	primum *Infans*, 1.
then a Boy, 2.	deinde *Puer*, 2.
then a Youth, 3.	tum *Adoleſcens*, 3.
then a Young-man, 4.	inde *Juvenis*, 4.
then a Man, 5.	poſteà *Vir*, 5.
after that, an Elderly-man, 6.	dehinc *Senex*, 6.
and at laſt,	tandem
a decrepid old Man, 7.	*Silicernium*. 7.
So alſo	Sic etiam
in the other ſex,	in altero Sexu,
there are, a Girle, 8.	ſunt, *Pupa*, 8.
A Damoſel, 9.	*Puella*, 9.
A Maid, 10.	*Virgo*, 10.
A Woman, 11.	*Mulier*, 11.
an Elderly Woman, 12.	*Vetula*, 12.
and a decrepid old Woman. 13.	*Anus* decrepita. 13.

Membra

XXXVIII.

The outward parts of a Man.

Membra Hominis Externa.

The Head, 1. is above, the Feet, 20. below.
The forepart of the Neck, (which ends at the Arm-holes 2.) is the Throat, 3. the hinder-part the Crag, 4.
The Breaſt, 5. is before; the back: 6. behind;

Caput 1. eſt ſuprà, infrà, *Pedes*, 20.
Colli (quod deſinit in *Axillas* 2.) pars anterior, eſt *Jugulum*; 3. poſterior, *Cervix*. 4.
Pectus, 5. eſt antè; retrò, *Dorſum*: 6.

women.

women have in it	in illo sunt Fœminis,
two Dugs 7.	binæ *Mammæ* 7.
with Nipples.	cum *Papillis.*
Under the breast	Sub pectore
is the Belly, 9.	est *Venter,* 9.
in the middle of it,	in ejus medio,
the Navel, 10.	*Umbilicus,* 10.
underneath the groyn, 11.	subtus *Inguen,* 11.
and the privities.	& *pudenda.*
The Shoulder-blades,	A tergo,
are behind the Back, 12.	sunt *Scapulæ,* 12.
on which the	à quibus pendent
Shoulders depend 13.	*Humeri,* 13.
on these the Arms 14.	ab his *Brachia,* 14.
with the Elbow, 15.	cum *Cubito,* 15.
and then the hands on either side,	inde, ad utrumque *latus,*
the right, 8.	*Manûs, Dextera,* 8.
and the left, 16.	& *Sinistra,* 16.
The next to the shoulders,	Humeros, excipiunt
are the Loyns 17.	*Lumbi* 17.
with the Hips, 18.	cum *Coxis,* 18.
and in the breech,	& in *Podice* (culo)
the Buttocks. 19.	*Nates.* 19.
These make the Foot;	*Pedem* absolvunt;
the Thigh, 21.	*Femur,* 21.
then the Leg, 23.	tum *Crus,* 23.
(the Knee being betwixt them 22.)	(intermedio *Genu* 22.)
in which is the Calf, 24.	in quo *Sura,* 24.
with the Shin, 25.	cum *Tibiâ,* 25
then the Anckles, 26.	abhinc *Tali,* 26.
the Heel, 27.	*Calx* (Calcaneum) 27.
and the Sole, 28.	& *Solum,* 28.
in the very end,	in extremo
the great Toe, 29.	*Hallux,* 29.
with four (other) Toes.	cum quatuor Digitis.

Caput

XXXIX.

The Head and the Hand. *Caput & Manus.*

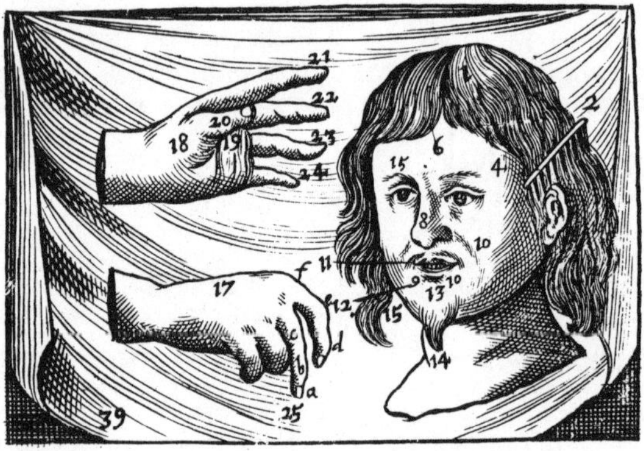

In the Head are,
the Hair, 1.
(which is Combed
with a Comb, 2.)
two Ears, 3.
the Temples, 4.
and the Face, 5.
In the Face are,
the Forehead, 6.
both the Eyes, 7.
the Nose, 8.
(with two Nostrils)
the Mouth, 9.

In *Capite* sunt
Capillus, 1.
(qui pectitur
Pectine 2.)
Aures 3. binæ,
& *Tempora*, 4.
Facies, 5.
In facie sunt
Frons, 6.
Oculus 7. uterque,
Nasus 8.
(duabus *Naribus*,)
Os, 9.

the

the Cheeks 10.	*Genæ* (Malæ) 10.
and the Chin. 13.	& *Mentum*. 13.
The Mouth is fenced	Os septum est
with a Mustacho, 11.	*Mystace*, 11.
and Lips; 12.	& *Labiis*; 12.
a Tongue and Palate,	*Lingua* cum *Palato*,
and Teeth 16.	*Dentibus* 16.
in the Cheek-bone.	in *Maxillâ*.
A Mans Chin is co-	Mentum virile
vered with a Beard; 14.	tegitur *Barbâ*; 14.
and the eye,	Oculus verò,
(in which is the white	(in quo *Albugo*
and the Apple)	& *Pupilla*)
with eye-lids,	*palpebris*
and an eye-brow. 15.	& *supercilio*. 15.
The Hand being	*Manus* contracta,
closed, is a Fist; 17.	*Pugnus* 17. est;
being open, is a	aperta,
palm, 18. (hollow 19.	*Palma*, 18.
in the midst, is the	in medio, *Vola*, 19.
of the Hand; the extre-	
mity is the Thumb, 20.	extremitas, *Pollex*, 20.
with four Fingers,	cum quatuor *Digitis*,
the fore-finger, 21.	*Indice*, 21.
the middle-finger, 22,	*Medio*, 22.
the Ring-finger, 23.	*Annulari*, 23.
and the little-finger, 24	& *Auriculari*. 24.
In every one are three	In quolibet
joynts a.b.c. (d.e.f.	sunt *articuli* tres *a.b.c.*
and as many knuckles	& totidem *Condyli d.e.f.*
with a Nail. 25.	cum *Ungue*. 25.

XL.

The Fleſh and the Bowels.

Caro & Viſcera.

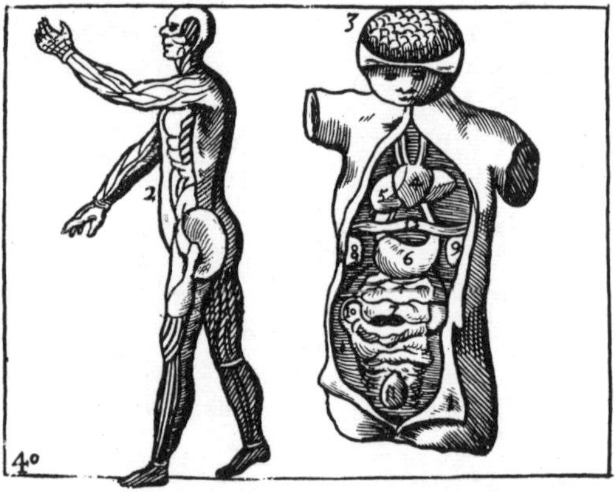

In the Body are the Skin with the Membranes, the fleſh with the muſcles, the Channels, the Griſtles, the bones & the bowels.

The Skin 1. being puld off, the fleſh 2 appeareth, not in a continued lump, but being distributed, as it were into ſtuft puddings which they call muſcles

In *Corpore* ſunt *Cutis* cum *Membranis*, *Caro* cum *Muſculis*, *Canales*, *Cartilagines*, *Oſſa* & *Viſcera*.

Detractâ *Cute* 1. apparet *Caro* 2. non continuâ maſſâ, ſed diſtributa, tanquam in farcimina, quos vocant *Muſculos*,

where-

whereof there are reckoned four hundred and five, being the	quorum numerantur *quadringenti quinque*
chanels of the Spirits	canales *Spirituum*
to move the members.	ad movendum *membra.*
The Bowels (bers:	*Viscera,*
are the inward mem-	sunt *membra* interna :
As, in the head the Brain 3.	Ut, in Capite, *Cerebrum* 3.
being compassed about with a Skull, and the skin which covereth the Skull.	circumdatum *Cranio* & *Pericranio.*
In the breast, the heart 4	In Pectore, *Cor* 4.
covered with a thin skin about it,	obvolutum *Pericardio*;
and the Lungs 5.	& *Pulmo* 5.
breathing to and fro.	respirans.
In the Belly,	In *Ventre,*
the Stomach 6.	*Ventriculus* 6.
and the Guts 7.	& *Intestina* 7.
covered with a Kell;	obducta *Omento*;
the Liver 8.	*Jecur* (Hepar) 8.
& on the left side oppo-	& à sinistro
site against it the milt 9	ei oppositus *Lien* 9.
the two kidneys 10.	duo *Renes* 10.
and the bladder 11.	cum *Vesicâ* 11.
The breast is	Pectus
divided from the belly	à Ventre dividitur
by a thick membrane,	crassâ membrana,
which is called the	quæ vocatur
Mid-riff 12.	*Diaphragma* 12.

XLI.

The Chanels and Bones. — *Canales & Ossa.*

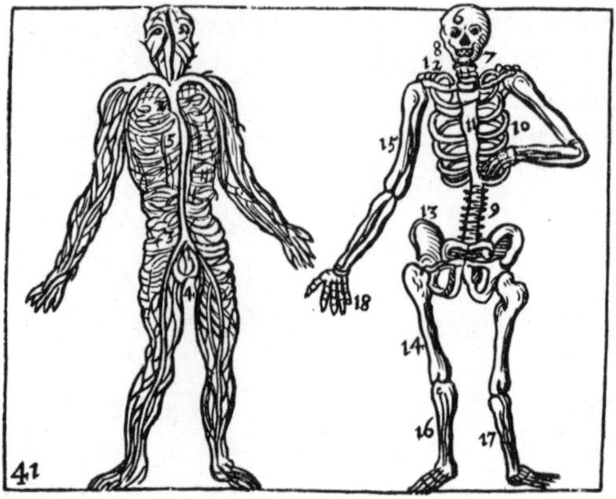

The Chanels of the body are, the Veins, carrying the blood from the Liver; (heat
The Arteries carrying and life from the heart;
The Nerves carrying sense and motion, throughout the body, from the brain.
You shall find these three, 1. (gether.
every where joyned to-
besides, from the mouth

Canales Corporis sunt *Venæ*, Sanguinem, ex Hepate;
Arteriæ, *calorem* & *Vitam*, è Corde;
Nervi, *Sensum* & *Motum*, à *Cerebro*, per Corpus deferentes.
Hæc tria, 1.
ubiq; sociata invenies.
Porrò, ab ore

into the ſtomach is the
Gullet 2.
the way of the meat
and drink : (Wezand 5.
and by it to the lights the
for breathing : from the
ſtomach to the arſe
is a great Gut 3.
to Purge out the Ordure ;
from the Liver to the Blad-
the Ureter 4. (der,
for making water.
The Bones are :
in the Head the Skull, 6.
the two Cheek-bones 7.
with thirty two Teeth, 8.
Then the back-bone, 9.
the Pillar of the body,
conſiſting of thirty four
turning-joynts, that the
body may bend it ſelf.
The Ribs, 10.
whereof there are XXIV.
The Breaſt-bone, 11.
the two Shoulder-blades, 12
the Buttock-bone, 13.
the bigger Bone
in the Arm, 15. (Arm,
and the leſſer-bone, in the
the Thigh-bone, 14.
the foremoſt, 16.
and the hindmoſt Bone,
in the Leg, 17.
The bones of the Hand 18.
are thirty four,
and of the Foot, 19. thirty.
The Marrow
is in the Bones.

in Ventriculum, *Gula*, 2.
via cibi ac Potûs ;
& juxtà hanc,
ad Pulmonem *Guttur*, 5.
pro reſpiratione ;
à ventriculo ad Anum,
Colon 3.
ad excernendum *Stercus* ;
ab Hepate ad Veſicam,
Uréter 4.
reddendæ Urinæ.
Oſſa ſunt :
in Capite, *Calvaria*, 6.
duæ *Maxillæ*, 7.
cum XXXII. *Dentibus* ;
Tum, *Spina dorſi*, 9.
corporis columna,
conſtans ex XXXIV.
Vertebris, ut Corpus
ſe flectere queat ;
Coſtæ, 10.
quarum viginti quatuor.
Os pectoris, 11.
duæ *Scapulæ*, 12.
Os Seſſibuli, 13.
Lacerti 15. & *Ulnæ*,
Tibiæ, 14.
Fibula 16, anterior
& poſterior, 17.
Oſſa *Manûs*, 18.
ſunt triginta quatuor,
Pedis, 19. triginta.
In Oſſibus
eſt *Medulla*.

XLII.

The outward and inward Senſes.	*Senſus externi & interni.*

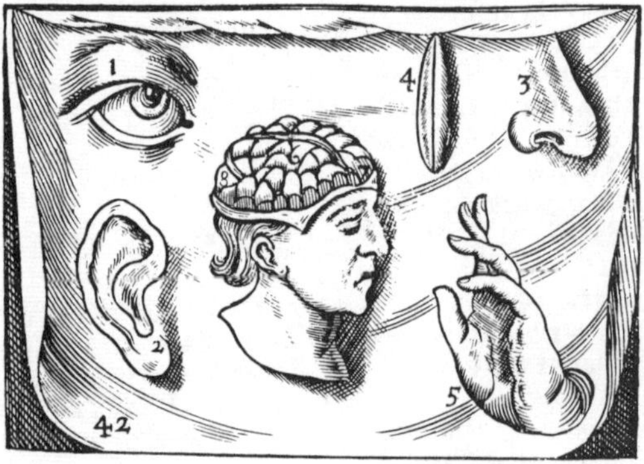

There are five outward Senſes ;	*Senſus* externi ſunt quinque ;
The Eye 1.	*Oculus* 1.
ſeeth colours,	videt *Colores*,
what is white or black,	quid album vel atrum,
green or blew,	viride vel cœruleum,
red or yellow.	rubrum aut luteum, ſit.
The Ear 2.	*Auris* 2.
heareth Sounds,	audit *Sonos*,
both natural,	tum naturales,
Voices and Words ;	Voces & Verba ;
and artificial,	tum artificiales,
muſical Tunes.	Tonos Muſicos.

The

The Noſe 3.
ſenteth ſmels
and ſtinks.
The Tongue 4.
with the root of the mouth
taſteth ſavours, what is
ſweet or bitter, keen or bi-
ſowr or harſh. (ting
The Hand 5.
by touching diſcerneth
the quantity
and quality of things,
the hot and cold,
the moiſt and dry,
the hard and ſoft,
the ſmooth and rough,
the heavy and light.
The inward Senſes
are three.
The Common-ſenſe 7.
under the forepart of the
apprehendeth (head,
things taken from the
outward Senſes.
The Phantaſie 6.
under the crown of the head
judgeth of thoſe things,
thinketh and dreameth.
The Memory 8.
under the hinder part of the
layeth up every thing (head
and fetcheth them out:
it loſeth ſome,
and this is forgetfulneſs.
Sleep,
is the Reſt of the Senſes.

Naſus 3.
olfacit Odores,
& Fætores
Lingua 4. cum Palato
guſtat Sapores,
quid dulce aut amarum,
acre aut acidum,
acerbum aut auſterum.
Manus 5.
dignoſcit tangendo
rerum Quantitatem
& Qualitatem,
calidum & frigidum,
humidum & ſiccum,
durum & molle,
læve & aſperum,
grave & leve.
Senſus interni
ſunt tres.
Senſus communis 7.
ſub *ſincipite*,
apprehendit
à Senſibus externis
perceptas res.
Phantaſia 6.
ſub *vertice*,
dijudicat res iſtas,
cogitat, ſomniat.
Memoria 8.
ſub *occipitio*,
ſingula recondit
& depromit:
quædam deperdit,
& hoc eſt *Oblivio*.
Somnus,
eſt Senſuum requies.

XLIII.

The *S*oul of man. *Anima hominis.*

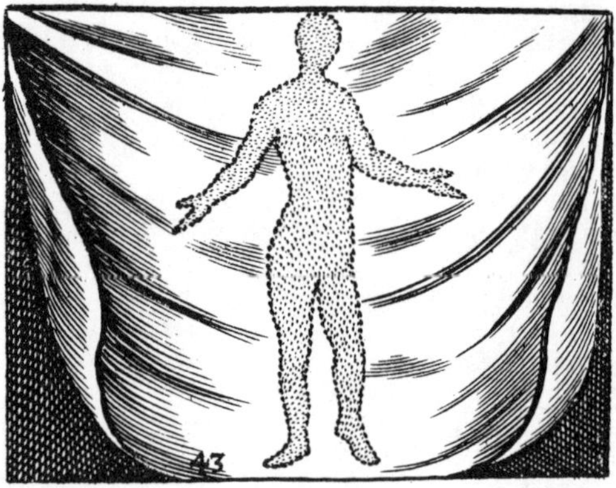

The Soul	*Anima*
is the life of the body,	eſt vita corporis,
one in the whole :	in toto una :
Only Vegetative	Tantùm *Vegetativa*,
in Plants ;	in *Plantis* ;
Withall ſenſitive	Simul *Senſitiva*,
in Animals ;	in *Animalibus* ;
And alſo Rational	Etiam *Rationalis*,
in Man.	in *Homine*.
This conſiſteth in	Hæc conſiſtit
three things ;	in tribus :
In the underſtanding	In *Mente* (Intellectu)

where-

whereby it judgeth,	quâ cognoscit,
and understandeth	& intelligit,
a thing good and evil,	Bonum ac Malum,
or true or apparent.	vel verum, vel apparens
In the Will,	In *Voluntate*,
whereby it chooseth,	quâ eligit,
and desireth,	& concupiscit,
or rejecteth	aut rejicit
or misliketh	& aversatur
a thing known.	cognitum.
In the Mind,	In *Animo*,
whereby it pursueth	quo prosequitur
the good chosen,	Bonum electum,
or avoideth the evil	vel fugit
rejected.	Malum rejectum.
Hence is Hope,	Hinc *Spes*,
and Fear,	& *Timor*,
in the desire	in cupidine
and dislike.	& aversatione.
Hence is Love	Hinc *Amor*
and Joy,	& *Gaudium*,
in the fruition :	in fruitione :
But Anger,	Sed *Ira*
and Grief,	ac *Dolor*,
in suffering.	in passione.
The true judgment of	Vera rei cognitio,
a thing is Knowledge ;	est *Scientia* ;
the false is Error, (on.	falsa, *Error*,
Opinion and Suspspici-	*Opinio*, *Suspicio*.

Deformes

XLIV.

Deformes & Monstrosi.

Deformed and Monstrous People.

Monſtrous
and deformed peop'e,
are thoſe which differ
in the body from the
ordinary ſhape; as are,
the huge Gyant, 1.
the little Dwarf, 2.
One with two bodies 3
One with two heads, 4.
and ſuch like Monſters.
Amongſt theſe are
reckoned,
The jolt headed, 5.
The great-Noſed, 6.
The blubber-lipped, 7.
The blub-cheeked, 8.
The goggle-eyed, 9.
The wry-necked, 10.
The great-throated, 11
The crump-backed, 12.
The crump-footed, 13.
The ſteeple-crown-
(ed, 15.
and to theſe
The bald-pated. 14.

Monſtroſi
& *Deformes* ſunt,
abeuntes corpore
à communi formâ:
ut ſunt,
immanis *Gigas*, 1.
nanus *Pumilio*, 2.
Bicorpor, 3.
Biceps, 4.
& id genus Monſtra.
His accenſentur:

Capito, 5.
Naſo, 6.
Labeo, 7.
Bucco, 8.
Strabo, 9.
Obſtipus, 10.
Strumoſus, 11.
Gibboſus, 12.
Loxipes, 13.
Cilo, 15.
adde
Calvaſtrum, 14.

XLV

The Dressing of Gardens. | *Hortorum cultura.*

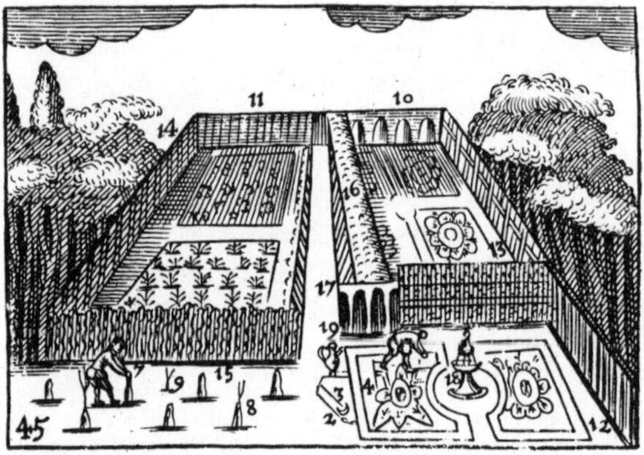

We have seen Man: Now let us go on to Mans living, and to Handy-craft-Trades, which tend to it.	Hominem vidimus: Jam pergamus ad *Victum* hominis, & ad *Artes Mechanicas*, quæ huc faciunt.
The first and most antient sustenance, were the fruits of the earth.	Primus & antiquissi- *Victus*, (mus *Terræ Fruges*.
Hereupon the first labour of Adam, was the dressing of a garden	Hinc primus Labor Adami, *Horti-cultura*.
The Gardiner 1. diggeth in a garden-plot,	*Hortulanus* (Olitor) 1 in *Viridario* fodit,

with

with a Spade 2.	*Ligone* 2.
or Mattock, 3.	aut *Bipalio*, 3.
and maketh Beds 4.	facitque *Pulvinos* 4.
and places wherein to plant Trees ; 5.	ac *Plantaria* ; 5.
on which he setteth	quibus infert
Seeds and Plants.	*Semina* & *Plantas*.
The Tree Gardiner 6.	*Arborator* 6.
	in *Pomario*
planteth Trees, 7.	plantat *Arbores*, 7.
in an Orchard,	inseritque
and grafteth ſiens 8.	*Surculos* 8.
in Stocks, 9.	*Viviradicibus*. 9.
He fenceth his Garden, either by Care,	Sepit Hortum, vel Cura,
with a mound, 10.	*Muro*, 10.
or a ſtone-wall, 11.	aut *Macerie*, 11.
or a rail, 12.	aut *Vacerrâ*, 12.
or Pales, 13.	aut *Plancis*, 13.
or a Hedge, 14.	aut *Sepe*, 14.
made of Hedge-ſtakes,	flexâ è *ſudibus*
and bindings ;	& *vitilibus* ;
Or by Nature, with Brambles and Bryars. 15	Vel Natura, *Dumis* & *Vepribus*. 15.
It is beautified	*Ambulacris* 16.
with Walks 16.	& *Pergulis* 17.
and Galleries. 17.	ornatur.
It is watered	*Fontanis* 18.
with Fountains 18.	& *Harpagio* 19.
and a watering-pot. 19.	rigatur.

Agri-

XLVI.

Husbandry. *Agricultura.*

The Plow-man 1.	*Arator* 1.
yoketh Oxen 3.	jungit *Boves* 3.
to a Plough, 2.	*Aratro*, 2.
and holdeth	&, tenens
the Plow-stilt, 4.	lævâ *Stivam*, 4.
in his left hand	
and the Plow-staff 5.	dextrâ *Rallam* 5.
in his right hand,	
(with which he re-	quâ amovet
moveth clods 6.)	*Glebas*, 6
he cutteth the Land	terram scindit
(which was manured	*Vomere*,
afore with Dung 8.)	& *Dentali*, 7.
with a Share, 7.	anteâ *Fimo* 8.
and a Coulter,	Surcoratam,

and

and maketh furrows. 9.	facitque *Sulcos*. 9.
Then he soweth the Seed 10.	Tum *seminat Semen* 10.
and harroweth it in with a Harrow. 11.	& innoccat *Occâ*. 11.
The Reaper 12. sheareth the Ripe Corn with a Sickle, 13.	*Messor* 12. metit fruges maturas *Falce messoriâ*, 13.
gathereth up the handfuls, 14.	colligit *Manipulos*, 14.
& bindeth the sheaves. (15.	& colligat *Mergetes*. 15.
The Thrasher 16. thrasheth Corn on the Barn floor 17. with a flayl, 18.	*Tritor* 16. in *areâ Horrei* 17. triturat Frumentum *Flagello* (tribulâ) 18.
tosseth it in a winnowing-basket, 19.	jactat *Ventilabro*, 19.
and so when the Chaff, and the Straw, 20. are separated from it,	atq; ita, separatâ *Paleâ* & *Stramine*, 20.
he putteth it into Sacks. (21.	congerit in *Saccos*, 21.
The Mower 22. maketh Hay in a Meadow, cutting down Grass with a Sithe, 23.	*Fœniseca* 22. in *Prato* facit *Fœnum*, desecans *Gramen Falce fœnariâ*, 23.
and raketh it together with a Rake, 24.	corraditq; *Rastro*, 24.
he maketh up cocks, 26	componit *Acervos* 26.
with a fork, 25.	*Furcâ*, 25.
& carrieth it on cariages (27. into the Hay-Barn. 28.	& convehit *Vehibus* 27. in *Fœnili*. 28.

Pecuaria

XLVII.

Grasing. | *Pecuaria.*

Tillage of ground, and keepping Cattle, was in old time the care of Kings & Noble-men, at this day only of the meanest sort of People.	*Agrorum cultus & res pecuaria*, antiquissimis temporibus, Regum, Heroum; hodie tantùm infimæ Plebis, Cura est.
The Neat-heard 1. calleth out the heards, 2. out of the beasthouses 3 with a Horn, 4. and driveth them to (feed	*Bubulcus* 1. evocat *Armenta* 2. è *Bovilibus* 3. *Buccinâ* (Cornu) 4. & pastum ducit.

The

The Shepherd 5.	*Opilio* (Pastor) 5.
feedeth his Flock 6.	pascit *Gregem*, 6.
being furnished with a Pipe 7.	instructus *Fistulâ* 7.
and a Scrip, 8.	& *Perâ*, 8.
and a Sheep-hook 9.	ut & *Pedo* 9.
having with him	habens secum
a great Dog 10.	*Molossum* 10.
fenced with a	munitum,
Collar 11.	contra Lupos,
against the Wolves.	*Millo.* 11.
Swine 12.	*Sues* 12.
are fed out of a	ex *haræ aqualiculo*
Swine-Trough.	saginantur.
The Farmers wife 13.	*Villica* 13.
milketh the Udder	mulget
of the Cow 14.	*vaccæ Ubera* 14.
at the Cratch 15.	ad *Præsepe* 15.
over a Milk-pale 16.	super *Mulctrâ* 16.
and maketh Butter of	& facit
Cream in a Churn 17.	in *Vase butyraceo* 17.
	Butyrum
	è *flore Lactis*,
and Cheeses 18.	& è *Coagulo*
of Curds.	*Caseos.* 18.
The Wool 19.	*Ovibus*
is shorn from Sheep,	detondetur *Lana* 19.
whereof several garments are made.	ex qua conficiuntur variæ *Vestes*.

XLVIII.

Mellificium.

The making of Honey.

The

The Bees ſend out a ſwarm 1. and ſet over it, a Leader 2.	*Apes* emittunt *Examen* 1. adduntque illi *Ducem* (Regem) 2.
That ſwarm, being ready to flie away is recalled by the tinkling of a Brazen veſſel 3. and is put up into a new Hive 4.	Examen illud, avolaturum, revocatur tinnitu *Vaſis ænei* 3. & includitur novo *Alveari* 4.
They make little Cells with ſix corners 5 and fill them with Honey-dew, and make Combs 6. out of which the Honey runneth 7.	Struunt *Cellulas* ſexangulares 5. eaſque complent *melligine*, & faciunt *Favos* 6. è quibus *Mel* effluit 7.
The Partitions being melted with fire, turn into Wax 8.	*Crates*, igne liquati, abeunt in *Ceram* 8.

XLIX.

Molitura.

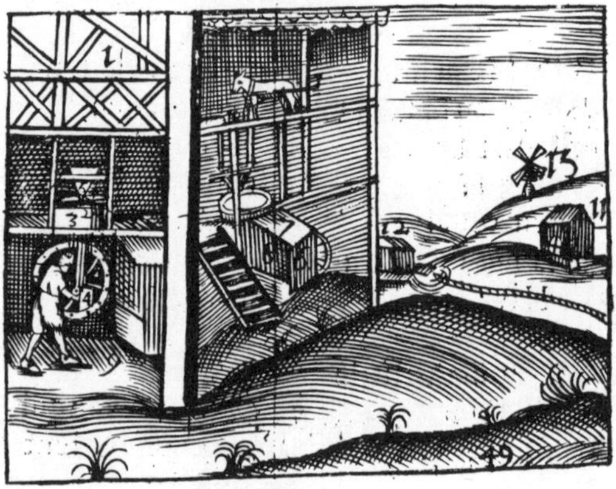

Grinding.

In

In a Mill 1.	In *Mola* 1.
A stone 2.	currit Lapis 2.
runneth upon a stone 3.	ſuper lapidem 3.
A Wheel 4.	circumagente
turning them about,	*Rota* 4.
and grindeth corn pou-	& conterit
red in by a Hopper 5.	per *Infundibulum* 5.
and parteth	infuſa Grana,
the Bran 6.	ſeparatque *Furfurem* 6.
falling into the	decidentem
Trough 7.	in *Ciſtam* 7.
from the Meal	à *Farinâ* (Polline)
slipping through	elabente
a Boulter 8.	per *Excuſſorium* 8.
Such a Mill,	Talis mola,
was first a	primum fuit,
Hand-mill 9.	*Manuaria* 9.
then a	deinde,
Horſe-mill 10.	*Jumentaria* 10.
then a Water-mill 11.	tum *aquatica* 11.
and a Ship-mill 12.	& *Navalis* 12.
and at last,	tandem,
a Wind-mill 13.	*Alata* (pneumatica) 13.

L.

Panificium.

Bread-Baking.

The Baker 1.	*Pistor* 1.
sifteth the Meal	cernit *Farinam*
in a Rindge 2.	*Cribro* 2. pollinario,
and putteth it into	& indit
the Kneading-trough 3.	*Mactra* 3.
Then he powreth	Tum affundit
water to it,	aquam,
and maketh Dough 4.	& facit *Massam* 4.
and kneadeth it	depsitque
with a wooden slice 5.	*spathâ* 5. ligneâ;
Then he maketh	Dein format
Loaves, 6.	*Panes* 6.
Cakes 7.	*Placentas* 7.
Cimnels 8.	*Similas* 8.
Rolls 9. *&c.*	*Spiras* 9 &c.
Afterwards he set-	Post imponit
teth them on a Peel 10.	*Pala* 10.
& putteth them thorow	& ingerit
the Oven-mouth 12.	*Furno* 11.
into the Oven 11.	per *Præfurnium* 12.
But first	Sed priùs
he pulleth out the fire,	eruit
and the coals with a	
Coal-Rake 13.	*Rutabulo* 13.
which he layeth on a	ignem & Carbones,
heap underneath 14.	quos infra congerit 14.
And thus	Et sic
is Bread baked,	pinsitur *Panis*,
having the Crust	habens extra
without 15.	*Crustam* 15.
& the Crumb within 16.	intus *Micam* 16.

LI.

Piſcatio.

Fiſhing.

The

The Fisher-man 1.	*Piscator* 1.
catcheth fish,	captat pisces,
either on the shoar,	sive, in littore,
with an Hook, 2.	*Hamo*, 2.
which hangeth by a line	qui ab *arundine*
from the angling-rod,	filo pendet,
and on which	& cui inhæret
the bait sticketh;	*Esca*;
or with a	sive
Cleek-Net, 3.	*Fundâ*, 3.
which hanging	quæ pendens
on a Pole, 4.	*Perticâ*, 4.
is put into the water;	aquæ immittitur;
or in a Boat, 5.	sive, in *Cymba*, 5.
with a Trammel-Net 6.	*Reti*, 6.
or with a Weel, 7.	sive *Nassa*, 7.
which is laid in	quæ per Noctem
the water by Night.	demergitur.

LII.

Fowling. *Aucupium.*

The Fowler 1.	*Auceps* 1.
maketh	exstruit
a bed, 2.	*Aream* 2.
spreadeth	superstruit illi
a Bird-net, 3.	*Rete* aucupatorium, 3.
throweth bait 4.	obsipat *Escam*, 4.
upon it, and hiding him-	&, abdens se
self in a Hut 5.	in *latibulo* 5.
he allureth Birds,	allicit aves,

by the chirping of	Cantu *Illicum*,
lure-birds, which partly	qui partim
hop upon the bed, 6.	in areâ currunt, 6.
and are partly	partim
shut in	Caveis
Cages, 7.	inclusi sunt, 7.
and thus he	atque ita
entangleth	reti obruit
Birds that flie over,	transvolantes
in his Net,	aves,
whilest they settle	dum
themselves down:	se demittunt:
or he setteth	aut tendit
Snares, 8.	*Tendiculas*, 8.
on which they hang,	quibus seipsas
and strangle	suspendunt
themselves;	& suffocant;
or he setteth	aut exponit
lime-Twigs 9.	*viscatos calamos* 9.
on a Perch, 10.	*Amiti*, 10.
upon which	quibus
if they sit,	si insident,
they enwrap their	implicant
Feathers,	Pennas,
that they cannot	ut nequeant
fly away, and fall	avolare,
down to the ground:	& decidunt in terram:
or he catcheth them	aut captat
with a Pole 11.	*Pertica*, 11.
and a Pit-fall 12.	vel *Decipula*. 12.

LIII.

Venatus.

Hunting.

The

The Hunter 1.	*Venator* 1.
hunteth wild-beasts,	venatur feras,
whilest he besetteth a	dum sylvam
Wood with Toyls, 2.	cingit *Cassibus*, 2.
stretched out	tentis
upon Shoars. 3.	super *Varos* (furcillas)
The Beagle 4.	*Canis sagax* 4.
traceth the wild-beast,	vestigat feram,
and findeth him out	aut indagat
by the sent;	odoratu;
the Tumbler,	*Vertagus* 5.
or Grayhound, 5.	persequitur.
pursueth it.	
The Woolf,	*Lupus*,
falleth into	incidit
a Pit; 6.	in *Foveam*; 6.
the Stag, 7.	fugiens *Cervus*, 7.
as he runneth away,	in *plagas*.
into Toyles.	
The Boar, 8.	*Aper*, 8.
is struck thorow with	transverberatur
a Hunting-Spear, 9.	*Venabulo*. 9.
The Bear 10.	*Ursus* 10.
is bitten	mordetur
by Dogs,	à canibus,
and is knocked	& tunditur
with a Club. 11.	*Clava*. 11.
If any thing get	Si quid effugit,
away, it escapeth, 12.	evadit, 12.
as here a Hare,	ut hîc *Lepus*
and a Fox.	& *Vulpes*.

Lanionia,

LIV.

Lanionia.

Butchery.

The

The Butcher, 1.	*Lanio* 1.
killeth	mactat
fat Cattle, 2.	*Pecudem altilem*, 2.
(The lean 3.	(*Vescula* 3.
are not fit to eat)	non sunt vesca)
he knocketh them	prosternit
down with an Ax, 4.	*Clava*, 4.
or cutteth their throat	vel jugulat
with a slaughter-knife 5	*Clunaclo*, 5.
he fleaeth them, 6.	
and cutteth them in	excoriat (deglubit) 6.
pieces, and hangeth out	dissecatque,
the flesh to sell	& carnes
in the Shambles 7.	in *Macello* 7.
	venum exponit.
He dresseth a swine 8.	*Suem* 8.
with fire,	glabrat igne,
or scalding water, 9.	vel aquâ fervidâ, 9.
& maketh gammons, 10.	& facit *Pernas*, 10.
Pestills 11.	*Petasones* 11.
and Flitches: 12.	& *Succidias*: 12.
Besides,	Præterea,
several Puddings,	*Farcimina* varia,
Chitterlings, 13.	*Faliscos*, 13.
Bloodings, 14.	*Apexabones*, 14.
Liverings, 15.	*Tomacula*, 15.
Sausages. 16.	*Botulos* (Lucanicas.) 16.
The Fat 17.	*Adeps* 17.
and Tallow 18.	& *Sebum* 18.
are melted.	eliquatur.

Coquinaria.

LV.

Cookery. *Coquinaria.*

The Yeoman of the Larder 1.	*Promus condus* 1.
bringeth forth Provision 2.	profert
out of the Larder. 3.	e *Penu* 3. *Obsonia.* 2.
The Cook 4. taketh them, and maketh several Meats.	Ea accipit *Coquus* 4. & coquit varia *esculenta.*
He first pulleth off the Feathers, and draweth the guts out of the Birds 5.	*Aves* 5. prius deplumat & exenterat;
He scaleth and splitteth Fish. 6.	*Pisces* 6. desquamat & exdorsuat;

He

He draweth some flesh with lard, by means of a Larding-Needle 7.	Quasdam carnes *lardo* trajectat, ope *Creacentri* 7.
He caseth Hares 8.	*Lepores* 8. exuit
Then he boyleth them in Pots 9. and Kettles 10. on the Hearth 11. and scummeth them with a Scummer 12.	Tum elixat *Ollis* 9. & *Cacabis* 10. in *Foco* 11. & despumat *Ligula* 12.
He seasoneth things that are boyled, with Spices, which he poundeth with a Pestil 14. in a Mortar 13. or grateth with a Grater 15.	Elixata condit aromatibus, quæ comminuit *Pistillo* 14. in *Mortario* 13. aut terit *Radulâ* 15.
He rosteth some on Spits 16. and with a Jack 17. or upon a Grid-iron 18.	Quædam assat *Verubus* 16. & *Automato* 17. vel super *Craticulam* 18.
Or fryeth them in a Frying-pan 19. upon a Brand-iron 20.	Vel frigit *Sartagine* 19. super *Tripodem* 20.
Kitchen Utensils besides are a Cole-Rake 21. a Chafing-Dish 22. a Trey 23. in which Dishes 24. and Platters 25. are washed; a pair of Tongs 26. a Shredding-Knife 27. a Colander 28. a Basket 29. and a Bezom 30.	*Vasa Coquinaria* prætereâ sunt *Rutabulum* 21. *Foculus* (Ignitabulum) 22. *Trua* 23. (in quâ eluuntur *Catini* 24. & *Patinæ* 25.) *Forniceps* 26. *Culter incisorius* 27. *Qualus* 28. *Corbis* 29. & *Scopæ* 30.

LVI.

The Vintage. | ***Vindemia.***

Wine	*Vinum*
groweth	creſcit
in the Vine-yard, 1.	in *Vinea*, 1.
where Vines	ubi *Vites*
are propagated,	propagantur,
and tied with	& viminibus
Twigs to Trees 2.	ad arbores, 2.
or to props, 3.	vel ad *Palos* (ridicas) 3.
or frames, 4.	vel ad *Juga*, 4.
	alligantur.
When the time of	Cum tempus
grape-gathering	vindemiandi adeſt,
is come, they cut off	abſcindunt

the

the Bunches,	*Botros*,
and carry them in	& comportant
meaſures of three	
buſhels 5.	*Trimodiis*, 5.
and throw them	conjiciuntque
into a Vat, 6.	in *Lacum*, 6.
and tread them with	
their Feet, 7.	calcant *pedibus*, 7.
or ſtamp them with a	aut tundunt
wooden Peſtill, 8.	*ligneo Pilo*, 8.
and ſqueeſe out the	& exprimunt
juice in the	ſuccum ·
Wine-preſs, 9.	*Torculari*, 9.
which is called muſt, 11.	qui dicitur *Muſtum*, ii.
and being received in	
a great Tub, 10.	&. *Orcâ* 10.
it is powred into	exceptum,
Hogſheads, 12.	*Vaſis* (Doliis) 12.
	infunditur,
it is ſtopped up 15.	operculatur, 15.
and being laid cloſe in	& in *Cellis*
Cellars upon ſettles 14.	ſuper *Cantherios* 14.
it becommeth wine.	abditum, in Vinum a-
It is drawn out of	E *dolio* (bit.
the Hogſhead,	promitur,
with a Cock, 13.	*Siphone*, 13.
or faucet, 16.	aut *Tubulo*, 16.
(in which is	(in quo eſt
a Spigot)	*Epiſtomium*)
the Veſſel being	Vaſe relito.
unbunged.	

LVII.

Zythopœia.

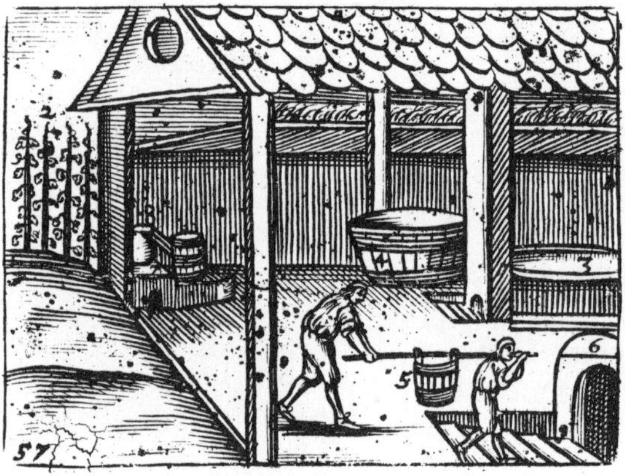

Brewing.

Where Wine is not to be had	Ubi non habetur *Vinum*, bibitur
they drink Beer,	*Cerevisia* (Zythus)
which is brewed	quæ
of Malt 1.	ex *Byne* 1.
and Hops, 2.	& *Lupulo*, 2.
in a Caldron 3.	in *Aheno* 3.
afterwards it is	coquitur;
powred into Vats, 4.	post in *Lacus*, 4.
and when it is cold	effunditur,
it is carried	&, frigefactum,
in Soes, 5.	*Labris* 5. defertur
into the Cellar 6.	in *Cellaria* 6.
and is put into	& vasibus
Vessels.	infunditur.
Brandi-wine,	*Vinum sublimatum*,
extracted by the power	è fecibus vini
of heat from dregs	in *Aheno*, 7.
of wine in a Pan, 7.	cui superimpositum est
over which	*Alembicum*, 8.
a Limbeck 8.	vi Caloris
is placed,	extractum,
droppeth through	destillat
a Pipe 9.	per *Tubum* 9.
into a Glass.	in *Vitrum*.
Wine and Beer,	Vinum & Cerevisia,
when they turn sowr,	acescens,
become Vinegar.	fit *Acetum*.
They make Mede	Ex Vino & Melle
of Wine and Honey.	faciunt *Mulsum*.

LVIII.

A Feast. *Convivium.*

When a Feast	Cum apparatur
is made ready,	*Convivium*,
the Table is covered	Mensa sternitur
with a Carpet 1	*Tapetibus* 1.
and a Table-Cloth 2.	& *Mappâ*, 2.
by the Waiters,	à *Triclinariis*,
who besides	qui præterea apponunt
lay the Trenchers, 3.	*Discos* (Orbes) 3.
Spoons, 4.	*Cochlearia*, 4.
Knives, 5.	*Cultros*, 5.
with little Forks, 6.	cum *Fuscinulis*, 6.
Table-Napkins, 7.	*Mappulas*, 7.
Bread, 8.	*Panem* 8.

with

with a Salt-sellar. 9.
Messes
are brought
in Platters, 10.
a Pie, 19.
on a Plate.
The Guests,
being brought in by
the Host 11.
wash their Hands
out of a Laver, 12.
or Ewer, 14.
over a Hand-Basin, 13.
or Bowl, 15.
and wipe them with
a Hand-Towel, 16.
then they sit at the Table
on Chairs. 17.
The Carver 18.
breaketh up the good cheer
and divideth it.
Sauces are set
amongst Roast-meat
in Sawsers. 20.
The Butler 21.
filleth strong wine
out of a Cruse 25.
or Wine-pot 26.
or Flagon, 27.
into Cups 22.
or Glasses 23.
which stand on
a Cup-board 24.
and he reacheth them
to the Master
of the Feast, 28.
who drinketh to his
Guests.

cum *Salino*. 9.
Fercula
inferuntur
in *Patinis*, 10.
Artocreas, 19.
in *Lance*.
Convivæ,
ab *Hospite*
introducti 11.
abluunt Manûs
è *Gutturnio* 12.
vel *Aquali*, 14.
super *Malluvium* 13.
aut *Pelvim*, 15.
terguntque
Mantili, 16.
tum assident Mensæ
per *Sedilia*. 17.
Structor 18.
deartuat dapes
& destribuit.
Assaturis
interponuntur
Embammata
in *Scutellis*. 20.
Pincerna 21.
infundit *Temetum*,
ex *Urceo* 25.
vel *Cantharo* 26.
vel *Lagena*, 27.
in *Pocula* 22.
& *Vitrea* 23.
quæ extant
in *Abaco* 24.
& porrigit
Convivatori, 28.
qui *Hospitibus* propinat.

LIX.

Tractatio Lini.

The dressing of Line.

Line and Hemp	*Linum* & *Cannabis,*
being rated in water,	aquis macerata,
and dried again, 1.	rurſumq; ſiccata, 1.
are braked with a	contunduntur
wooden Brake, 2.	*Frangibulo ligneo,* 2.
where the Shives 3.	(ubi *Cortices* 3.
fall down, then they	decidunt)
are heckled with an	tùm carminantur
Iron Heckle, 4.	*Carmine ferreo,* 4.
where the Tow 5.	ubi *Stupa* 5.
is parted from it.	ſeparatur.
Flax is tied to	*Linum purum*
a Diſtaff, 6.	alligatur *Colo,* 6.
by the Spinſter, 7.	à *Netrice,* 7.
which with her left	quæ ſiniſtrâ
hand pulleth out	
the Thred, 8.	trahit *filum,* 8.
and with her right	dexterâ 12.
hand turneth a wheel 9.	*Rhombum* (girgillum) 9.
or a Spindle 10.	vel *Fuſum* 10.
upon which is	(in quo
a Wharl 11.	*Verticillus* 11.) verſat.
The Spool receiveth	Fila accipit,
the Thred, 13.	*Volva,* 13.
which is drawn thence	inde deducuntur
upon a Yarn-windle; 14.	in *Alabrum*; 14.
hence either Clewes 15.	hinc vel *Glomi* 15.
are wound up	glomerantur,
or Hanks 16.	vel *Faſciuli* 16.
are made.	fiunt.

Textura.

LX.

Textura.

Weaving.

The

The Webster,	*Textor*,
undoeth the Clewes, 1.	diducit in *Stamen*
into Warp,	*Glomos*, 1.
and wrappeth it about	& circumvolvit
the Beam, 2.	*Jugo*, 2.
and as he sitteth	ac sedens
in his Loom, 3.	in *Textrino*, 3.
he treadeth upon	pedibus
the Treddles, 4.	calcat
with his Feet.	*Insilia*. 4.
He divideth	*Liciis*
the warp, 5. with yarn,	diducit *Stamen*, 5.
and throweth	& trajicit
the Shuttle 6.	*Radium*, 6.
thorow, in which is	in quo est
the Woose,	*Trama*,
and striketh it close	ac densat
with the sley, 7.	*Pectine*, 7.
and so maketh	atque ita conficit
Linnen-cloth. 8.	*Linteum*. 8.
So also the	Sic etiam
Clothier	*Pannifex*
maketh Cloth	facit *Pannum*
of Wooll.	è *Lanâ*.

Lintea

LXI.

Lintea.

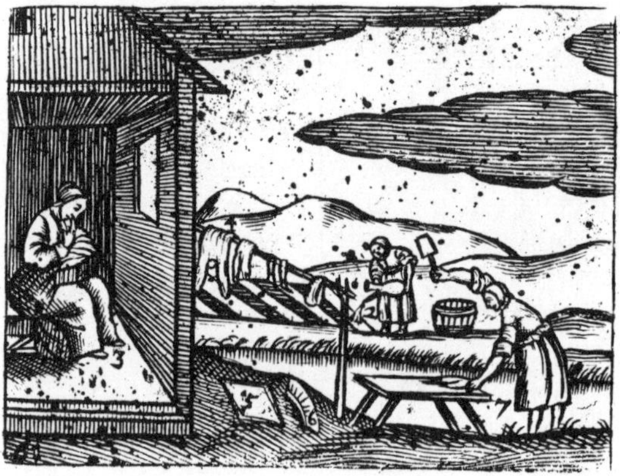

Linnen-Clothes.

Lin-

Linnen-webs	*Linteamina*
are bleached in the (Sun 1.	insolantur 1.
with water poured on them 2.	aquâ perfusa 2.
till they be white.	donec candefiant.
Of them	Ex iis
the Sempster 3.	*Sartrix* 3.
soweth Shirts 4.	suit *Indusia* 4.
Hand-kirchers 5.	*Muccinia* 5.
Bands 6.	*Collaria* 6.
Caps, *&c.*	*Capitia*, &c.
These,	Hæc,
if they be fouled,	si sordidentur,
are washed again by the Landress 7.	à *Lotrice* 7. rursum lavantur
in water	
or Lee,	aquâ sive *lixivio*
and Sope.	ac *Sapone*.

Sartor

LXII.

Sartor.

The Taylor.

The

The Taylor 1.	*Sartor* 1.
cutteth Cloth 2.	discindit *Pannum* 2.
with Shears 3.	*Forfice* 3.
and soweth it together	consuitque,
with a Needle	*Acu*
and double thred 4.	& *filo duplicato* 4.
Then he	Posteâ
presseth the Seams	complanat *Suturas*
with a pressing-iron 5.	*Ferramento* 5.
And thus he maketh	Sicque conficit
Coats 6.	*Tuninas* 6.
with Plaits 7.	*Plicatas* 7.
in which the	in quibus infra est
Border 8.	*Fimbria* 8.
is below with Laces 9.	cum *Institis* 9.
Cloaks 10.	*Pallia* 10.
with a Cape 11.	cum *Patagio* 11.
and Sleeve Coats 12.	& *Togas manicatas* 12.
Doublets 13.	*Thoraces* 13.
with Buttons 14.	cum *Globulis* 14.
and Cuffs 15.	& *Manicis* 15.
Breeches 16.	*Caligas* 16.
sometimes	aliquando
with Ribbons 17.	cum *Lemniscis* 17.
Stockings 18.	*Tibialia* 18.
Gloves 19.	*Chirothecas* 19.
Muntero Caps 20, *&c.*	*Amiculum* 20, &c.
So the Furrier	Sic *Pellio*,
maketh Furred garments	facit *Pellicia*,
of Furs.	è *Pellibus*.

LXIII.

Sutor.

The Shoo-maker.

The

The Shoo-maker 1.
maketh Slippers 7.
Shooes 8.
(in which is seen
above the
upper-Leather,
beneath
the Sole,
and on both sides
the Latchets)
Boots 9.
and High-Shooes 10.
of Leather, 5.
(which is
cut with a
Cutting-Knife 6.)
by means of
an Awl 2.
and Lingel 3.
upon a
Last 4.

Sutor 1.
conficit,
ope *Subulæ* 2.
& *fili picati* 3.
ſuper *Modulo* 4.
è *Corio* 5.
(quod
Scalpro ſutorio 6.
diſcinditur)
Crepidas (*Sandalia*) 7.
Calceos 8.
(in quibus
ſpectatur
ſupernè
Obſtragulum,
infernè
Solea,
& utrinque
Anſa)
Ocreas 9.
& *Perones* 10.

LXIII.

The Carpenter. *Faber lignarius.*

We have seen
Mens Food
and cloathing :
now his dwelling
followeth.

At first they dwelt
in Caves 1.
then in
Booths
or Huts 2.
and then again
in Tents 3.
at the last
in Houses.

Hominis
Victum & Amictum,
vidimus :
sequitur nunc,
Domicilium ejus.

Primò habitabant
in *Specubus* 1.
deinde
in *Tabernaculis*
vel *Tuguriis* 2.
tum etiam
in *Tentoriis* 3.
demum,
in *Domibus*.

The Woodman fel-	*Lignator*
leth and heweth down	*Securi* 4.
Trees 5.	ſternit & truncat
with an Ax 4.	*Arbores* 5.
the Boughs 6.	remanentibus
remaining.	*Sarmentis* 6.
He cleaveth Knotty	*Clavoſum Lignum*
with a Wedg 7. (wood	findit *Cuneo* 7.
which he forceth in	quem adigit
with a Beetle 8.	*Tudite* 8.
and maketh	& componit
Wood-ſtacks. 9.	*Strues* 9.
The Carpenter	*Faber Lignarius*
ſquareth Timber with	aſciat *Aſciâ* 10.
a Chip-Ax 10.	Materiam,
whence Chips 11.	unde cadunt
fall, (Saw 12.	*Aſſulæ* 11.
and ſaweth it with a	& ſerrat *Serra* 12.
where the Saw duſt 13.	ubi *Scobs* 13.
falleth down.	decidit.
Afterwards he lifteth	Poſt elevat *tignum*
the beam upō treſſels 14.	ſuper *Canterios* 14.
by the help of a Pully 15.	ope *Trochleæ* 15.
faſteneth it with	
Cramp-irons 16.	affigit *Anſis* 16.
and marketh it out	& lineat
with a Line 17.	*Amuſſi* 17.
Then he frameth	Tum compaginat
the Walls together, 18	*Parietes* 18.
and faſtneth the great	& configit *trabes*
pieces with pins. 19.	*Clavis trabalibus* 19.

LXIV

Faber Murarius.

The Mason.

The

The Mason 1. layeth a Foundation, and buildeth Walls 2.	*Faber Murarius* 1. ponit *Fundamentum* & ſtruit *Muros* 2.
Either of Stones, which the Stone-digger getteth out of the Quarry 3. and the Stone-cutter 4. ſquareth by a Rule 5.	Sive e *Lapidibus* quos *Lapidarius* eruit in *Lapicidinâ* 3. & *Latomus* 4. conquadrat ad *Normam* 5.
Or of Bricks 6. which are made of Sand and Clay ſteeped in water, and are burned with fire.	Sive e *Lateribus* 6. qui, ex *arenâ* & *luto*, aquâ intritis, formantur, & igne excoquuntur.
Afterwards he plai- ſtereth it with Lime, by means of a Trowel 7 and garniſheth it with Rough caſt 8.	Dein cruſtat *Calce*, ope *Trullæ* 7. & *Tectorio* veſtit 8.

LXV.

Machinæ.

Engines.

One

One can carry as much by thrusting a Wheel-Barrow 3. afore him, having an Harness 4. hanged on his neck, as two can carry on a Cole-staff 1. or Hand-barrow 2.	Quantum duo ferre *Palangâ* 1. (possunt, vel *Feretro* 2. tantum potest unus, trudendo ante se *Pabonem* 3. suspensâ à collo *Ærumnâ* 4.
But he can do more that rolleth a weight, laid upon Rollers 6. with a Lever 5.	Plus autem potest, qui molem, *Phalangis* (Cylindris) 6. impositam, provolvit, *Vecte* 5.
A Wind-Beam 7. is a post which is turned by going about it.	*Ergáta* 7. est columella, quæ versatur circumeundo.
A Crane 8. hath a hollow-wheel, in which one walking, draweth weights out of a Ship, or letteth them down into a Ship.	*Geranium* 8. habet *Tympanum*, cui inambulans quis, pondera navi extrahit, aut in navem demittit.
A Rammer 9. is used to fasten Piles 10. it is lifted up with a rope drawn by Pulor with hands, (lies 11. if it have handles 12.	*Fistuca* 9. adhibetur ad pangendum *Sublicas* 10. adtollitur, fune, tracto per *Trochleas* 11. vel manibus, si *ansas* habet 12.

LXVI.

A House. Domus.

The Porch 1. (house.
is before the door of the
The door hath
a threshold 3.
and a Lintel 2.
and Posts 4.
on both sides
The Hindges 5.
are on the right hand
upon which the doors 6
hang,
the Latch 7.
and the Bolt 8.
are on the left hand.
Before the house
is a fore-court 9.

Ante *Jannam Domûs*
est *Vestibulum* 1.
Janna habet
Limen 2.
& *Superliminare* 3.
& utrinque
Postes 4.
A dextris
sunt *Cardines* 5.
à quibus pendent
Fores 6.
à sinistris *Claustrum* 7.
aut *Pessulus* 8.

Sub ædibus
est *Cavædium* 9.

with

with a Pavement of
ſquare-ſtones, 10.
born up with pillars, 11.
in which is the
Chapiter 12.
and the Baſe. 13.
They go up into the
upper-ſtories
by Greeſes, 14.
and winding-ſtairs 15.
The Windows, 16.
appear on the outſide,
and the Grates 17.
the Galleries, 18.
the water-Tables, 19.
and Buttereſſes 20.
to bear up the Walls.
On the Top
is the Roof, 21.
covered with Tyles, 22.
or Shingles, 23.
which lye upon
Laths, 24. (25.
and theſe upon Rafters.
The Eaves, 26.
adhere to the Roof.
The place without
a Roof is called an
open Gallery. 27.
In the Roof are
Jutings out 28. (knops)
and Pinnacles 29. (or

pavimento teſſellato, 10.
fulcitum *columnis*, 11.
in quibus
Periſtylium 12.
& *Baſis* 13.
Per *Scalas* 14.
& *Cochlidia* 15. (res
aſcenditur in ſuperio-
contignationes.
Extrinſecus
apparent *Feneſtræ*, 16.
& *Cancelli* (clathra) 17.
Pergulæ, 18.
Suggrundia, 19.
& *Fulcra* 20.
fulciendis muris.
In ſummo eſt
Tectum, 21 [*tegulis*] 22.
contectum *Imbricibus*
vel *Scandulis*, 23.
quæ incumbunt
Tigillis, 24.
hæc *Tignis*. 25.
Tecto adhæret
Stillicidium. 26.
Locus ſine tecto
dicitur *Subdiale*. 27.
In tecto ſunt
Meniana 28.
& *Coronides*. 29.

Metalli-

LXVII.

Metallifodina.

A Mine.

Miners

Miners 1.	*Metalli-fossores* 1.
	ingrediuntur
go into the Grove, 2.	*Puteum fodinæ*, 2.
by a Stick, 3.	*Bacillo*, 3.
or by Ladders, 4.	sive *Gradibus*, 4.
with Lanthorns, 5.	cum *Lucernis*, 5.
and dig out the Oar,	& effodiunt
with a Pick, 6.	*Ligone*, 6.
which being put	*terram Metallicam*,
into Baskets, 7.	quæ imposita *Corbibus*, 7
is drawn out	
with a Rope 8.	extrahitur *Fune* 8.
by the means of	ope *Machinæ tractoriæ*,
a Turn, 9.	& defertur (9.
and is carried to the	
Melting-house, 10.	in *Ustrinam*, 10.
where it is forced	ubi igne urgetur,
with fire that the Metal	ut profluat
may run out, 12.	*Metallum*, 12.
the Dross, 11.	*Scoria*, 11.
is thrown aside.	seorsim abjiciuntur.

LXVIII.

Faber Ferrarius.

The Black-Smith.

The Black-Smith 1.	*Faber ferrarius* 1.
in his Smithie	
(or forge) 2.	in *Ustrinâ* (Fabricâ) 2.
bloweth the fire with a	inflat ignem
pair of Bellows, 3.	*Folle*, 3.
which he bloweth	quem adtollit
with his Feet, 4.	*Pede*, 4.
and so he heateth the	atque ita candefacit
Iron;	Ferrum;
And then he taketh	Deinde
it out with the tongs, 5.	eximit *Forcipe*, 5.
layeth it upon	imponit
the Anvile, 6.	*Incúdi*, 6.
and striketh it with	& cudit
a Hammer, 7.	*Malleo*, 7.
where the Sparks 8.	ubi *Strictura* 8.
flie off.	exiliunt.
And thus	Et sic
are hammered out	excuduntur
Nails, 9.	*Clavi*, 9.
Horshooes, 10.	*Solea*, 10.
Cart-strakes, 11.	*Canthi*, 11.
Chains, 12.	*Catena*, 12.
Plates,	*Lamina*,
Locks and Keys,	*Sera* cum *Clavibus*,
Hindges, &c.	*Cardines*, &c.
He quencheth	Ferramenta canden-
Hot-Irons	restinguit (tia
in the Cool-trough.	in *Lacu*.

Scriniarius

LXIX.

Scriniarius & Tornator.

The Box-maker, and the Turner.

The Box-maker, 1.	*Arcularius* 1.
smootheth	
hewen-boards 2.	edolat *Asseres* 2.
with a Plain, 3.	*Runcinâ*, 3.
upon a work board, 4.	in *Tabulâ*, 4.
he maketh them very	
smooth with	deplanat
a little plain, 5.	*Planulâ*, 5.
he boareth them thorow	perforat (terebrat)
with an augre, 6.	*Terebrâ*, 6.
carveth them with	sculpit
a Knife, 7.	*Cultro*, 7.
fasteneth them toge-	combinat
ther with Glew,	*Glutine*
and Cramp-Irons, 8.	& *Subscudibus*, 8.
and maketh	& facit
Tables, 9.	*Tabulas*, 9.
Boards, 10.	*Mensas*, 10.
Chests 11. *&c.*	*Arcas* (Cistas) 11. &c.
The Turner 12. (13.	*Tornio* 12.
sitting over the treddle	sedens in *Insili*, 13.
turneth with	
a throw, 15. (14.	tornat *Torno*, 15.
upon a Turners Bench,	super *Scamno* tornato (rio 14.
Bowls, 16.	*Globos*, 16.
Tops, 17.	*Conos* 17.
Puppets, 18.	*Icunculas* 18.
and such like	& similia
Turners work.	*Toreumata*.

Figulus.

LXX.

Figulus.

The Potter.

The

The Potter, 1.	*Figulus*, 1.
sitting over	sedens
a Wheel, 2.	super *Rotâ*, 2.
maketh Pots, 4.	format ex *Argillâ*, 3.
Pitchers, 5.	*Ollas*, 4.
Pipkins, 6.	*Urceos*, 5.
Platters, 7.	*Tripodes*, 6.
Pudding-Pans, 8.	*Patinas*, 7.
Juggs, 9.	*Vasa testacea*, 8.
Lids, 10. *&c.*	*Fidelias*, 9.
of Potters-clay, 3. after-	*Opercula*, 10. &c.
wards he baketh them	postea excoquit
in an Oven, 11.	in *Furno*, 11.
and glazeth them	& incrustat
with White-Lead.	*Lithargyro*.
A broken Pot	Fracta Olla,
affordeth	dat
Pot-sheards. 12.	*Testas*, 12.

LXXI.

Partes Domûs.

The Parts of a Houſe.

A House is divided	*Domus* distinguitur
into inner Rooms,	in *Conclavia*,
such as are,	ut sunt,
the Entry, 1.	*Atrium*, 1.
the Stove, 2.	*Hypocaustum*, 2.
the Kitchin, 3.	*Culina*, 3.
the Buttery, 4.	*Cella penuaria*, 4.
the Dining Room, 5.	*Cœnaculum*, 5.
the Gallery, 6.	*Camera*, 6.
the Bed-chamber, 7.	*Cubiculum* 7.
with a Privy made	cum adstructo
by it, 8.	Secessu (*Latrinâ*) 8.
Baskets 9.	*Corbes* 9.
are of use for carrying	inserviunt
things to and fro;	rebus transferendis;
and Chests, 10.	*Arcæ*, 10.
(which are made fast	(quæ *Clave* 11.
with a Key) 11.	recluduntur)
for keeping them.	adservandis illis.
The Floor is under	Sub recto est
the Roof 12.	*Solum* [pavimentum]
In the Yard, 13.	In *Areâ*, 13, (12.
is a Well, 14.	*Puteus*, 14.
a Stable, 15.	*Stabulum* 15.
and a Bath. 16.	cum *Balneo*. 16.
Under the House,	Sub Domo,
is the Cellar. 17.	est *Cella*. 17.

LXXII.

Hypocaustum cum Dormitorio.

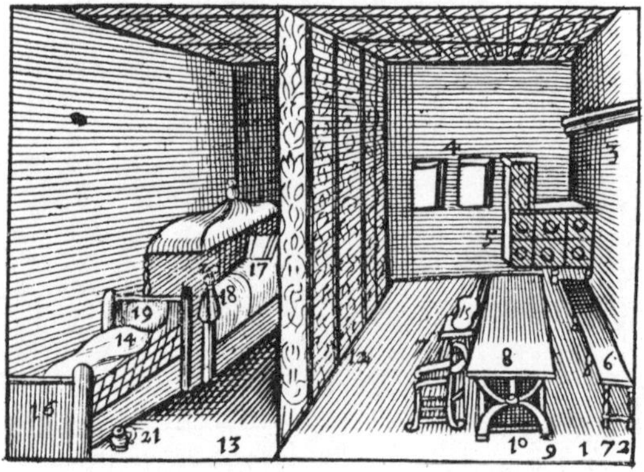

The Stove, with the Bed-Room.

The Stove 1.	*Hypocauſtum* 1.
is beautified with an	ornatur *Laqueari* 2.
Arched-Roof 2.	& *Parietibus*,
& wainſcotted walls, 3.	*tabulatis*, 3.
It is enlighted with	Illuminatur
Windows; 4.	*Feneſtris*; 4.
It is heated with	Calefit
an Oven. 5.	*Fornace*. 5.
Its Utenſils are,	Ejus Utenſilia ſunt,
Benches, 6.	*Scamna*, 6.
Stools, 7.	*Sellæ*, 7.
Tables, 8.	*Menſæ*, 8.
with Treſſels, 9.	cum *fulcris*, 9.
Footſtools, 10.	ac *ſcabellis*. 10.
and Cuſhions. 11.	& *Culcitris*. 11.
There are alſo	Appenduntur etiam
Tapeſtry hanged. 12.	*Tapetes*. 12.
For ſoft lodging,	Pro levi cubâtu,
in a ſleeping-room, 13.	in *Dormitorio*, 13.
there is a Bed 14.	eſt *Lectus*, (Cubile) 14.
ſpread on	ſtratus
a Bed-ſtead, 15.	in *Spondâ*, 15.
upon a Straw-pad, 16.	ſuper *Stramentum*, 16.
with Sheets, 17.	cum *Lodicibus*, 17.
and Cover-lids, 18.	& *Stragulis*, 18.
The Bolſter 19.	*Cervical* 19.
is under ones head.	eſt ſub capite.
The Bed is covered	*Canopéo* 20.
with a Canopy. 20.	Lectus tegitur.
A Chamber-Pot, 21.	*Matula* 21.
is for making water.	eſt veſicæ levandæ.

LXXIII.

Putei.

Wells.

Where

Where Springs	Ubi *Fontes*
are wanting,	deficiunt,
Wells are digged, 1.	effodiuntur *Putei*, 1.
& they are compassed	& circumdantur
about with a	
Brandrith, 2.	*Crepidine*, 2.
lest any should fall in.	ne quis incidat.
Thence is water	Inde hauritur aqua
drawn with Buckets 3.	*Urnis* (*situlis*) 3.
hanging either at	pendentibus
a Pole, 4.	vel *Perticâ*, 4.
or a Rope, 5.	vel *Fune*, 5.)
or a Chain; 6.	vel *Catenâ*, 6.
and that either	idque
by a swipe, 7.	aut *Tollenone*, 7.
or a windle, 8.	aut *Girgillo*, 8.
or a Turn, 9.	aut *Cylindro*, 9.
with a handle,	*manubriato*,
or a wheel, 10.	aut *Rotâ* (tympano)10.
or to conclude	aut denique
by a Pump. 11.	*Antliâ*, 11.

LXXIV.

Balneum.

The Bath.

He that desireth to be washt in cold water, goeth down into a river 1.
In a Bathing-house 2. we wash off the filth either sitting in a Tub 3. or going up into the Hot-house 4. and we are rubbed with a Pumice stone 6. or a Hair cloth 5. (7.
In the stripping room we put off our clothes, and have an Apron tied about us 8.
We cover our head with a Cap 9. and put our feet in a Basin 10.
The Bath-Woman 11. reacheth water in a Bucket 12. (13. drawn out of the trough into which it runneth out of Pipes. 14.
The Bath-keeper 15. lanceth with a Lancer, and by applying (16. Cupping Glasses 17. he draweth the blood betwixt the skin & the flesh, which he wipeth away with a Spung 18.

Qui lavari cupit aquâ frigidâ, descendit in *fluvium* 1.
In *Balneario* 2. abluimus *squalores*, sive sedentes in *Labro* 3. sive conscendentes in *Sudatorium* 4. (6. & defricamur *Pumice* aut *Cilicio* 5.
In *Apodyterio* 7. vestes exuimus, & præcingimur *Castulâ* (Subligari) 8.
Caput tegimus *Pileolo* 9 & pedes imponimus *Pelluvio* 10.
Balneatrix 11. ministrat aquam *Situlâ* 12. haustam ex *Alveo* 13. in quem defluit è *Canalibus* 14.
Balneator 15. scarificat *Scalpro* 16. & applicando *Cucurbitas* 17. extrahit *Sanguinem* subcutaneum, (18. quem abstergit *Spongiâ*

Ton-

LXXV.

Tonſtrina.

The Barbers-ſhop.

The Barber 1.
in the Barbers shop 2.
cutteth off
the Hair and the Beard
with a pair of Sizzars 3.
or shaveth with
a Razor,
which he taketh out of
his Case 4.
and he washeth
one over a Basen, 5.
with Suds
running out of
a Laver, 6.
and also with Sope, 7.
and wipeth him
with a Towel, 8.
combeth him with
a Comb, 9.
and curleth him with
a Crisping-Iron 10.
Sometimes he cutteth a vein with
a Pen-knife 11.
where the blood
spirteth out. 12.
The Chirurgion
cureth Wounds.

Tonsor 1.
in *Tonstrinâ* 2.
tondet
Crines & *Barbam*
Forpice 3.
vel radit
Novaculâ,
quam è *Thecâ* 4.
depromit;
& lavat
super *Pelvim*, 5.
Lixivio
defluente
e *Gutturnio*, 6.
ut & *Sapone*, 7.
& tergit
Linteo, 8.
pectit
Pectine, 9.
crispat
Calamistro 10.
Interdum
Venam secat
Scalpello 11.
ubi Sanguis
propullulat. 12.
Chirurgus,
curat *Vulnera*.

LXXVI.

Equile.

The Stable.

The Horse Keeper 1.	*Stabularius* (Equiso 1.)
cleanseth the Stable	purgat à *fimo* 2.
from Dung, 2.	*Stabulum*;
He tyeth a Horse 3.	Alligat *Equum* 3.
with a Halter 4.	*Capistro* 4.
to the Manger, 5.	ad *Præsepe*, 5.
or if he be apt to bite,	aut, si mordax sit,
he maketh him fast	constringit
with a Muzzel 6.	*Fiscellâ* 6.
Then he streweth	Deinde
Litter 7. under him.	substernit *stramenta* 7.
He winnoweth	*Avenam*
Oats with a Van 8.	*ventilat vanno* 8.
the Provender being	(paleis mixtâ,
mixt with Chaff, and	ac depromptâ
taken out of a Chest 10.	e *cistâ pabulatoriâ*) 10.
and feedeth the Horse	
with them, as also	eâque pascit equum,
with Hay 9.	ut & *Fœno* 9.
Afterwards he leadeth	Postea
him to the watering-	aquatum ducit
trough 11. to water.	ad *Aquarium* 11.
Then he rubbeth	Tum detergit
him with a Cloth 12.	*panno* 12.
combeth him with	
a Curry comb 15.	depectit *Strigili* 15.
covereth him with an	insternit
Housing Cloth 14.	*Gausape*, 14.
and looketh upon his	& *Soleas* inspicit,
Hoofs, whether	an *Calcei ferrei* 13.
the Shooes 13.	firmis *clavis* hæreant.
be fast with the nayls.	

Horo-

LXVII.

Horologia.

Dialls.

A

A Dial	*Horologium*
measureth hours :	dimetitur Horas.
A Sun Dial 1.	*Solarium* 1.
sheweth by the shadow	ostendit umbrâ
of the Cock 2.	*Gnomonis* 2.
what a Clock it is ;	quota sit hora ;
either on a wall,	sive in pariete, (*câ* 3.
or a Compass 3.	sive in *pyxide magneti-*
An hour-glass 4.	*Clepsydra* 4.
sheweth (hour,	ostendit
the four parts of an	partes horæ quatuor,
by the runing of sand,	fluxu *arenæ*,
heretofore of water.	olim aquæ.
A Clock 5.	*Autómaton* 5.
numbereth also the	numerat etiam
hours of the night,	nocturnas horas,
by the turning of the	circulatione rotarum,
wheels, the greatest	quarum maxima
whereof is drawn by	trahitur
a weight 6.	à *Pondere* 6.
and draweth the rest.	& trahit cæteras :
Then	Tum
either the	horam indicat,
Bell 7.	vel *Campana* 7.
by its sound,	sonitu suo,
being struck	percussa
on by the hammer,	à *malleolo* :
or the hand 8.	vel extrà
without, by its moti-	
on about, sheweth the	*Index* 8.
hour.	Circuitione suâ.

LXXVIII.

Pictura.

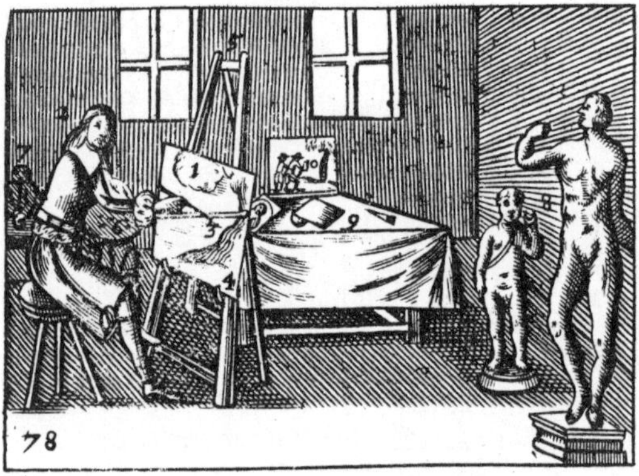

The Picture.

Pictures 1.	*Pictura* 1.
delight the eyes,	oblectant Oculos,
and adorn Rooms.	& ornant conclavia.
The Painter, 2.	*Pictor*, 2.
painteth an Image	pingit *effigiem*
with a Pencil, 3.	*Penicillo*, 3.
in a Table, 4.	in *Tabulâ*, 4.
upon a Caſe-frame ; 5.	ſuper *Pluteo* ; 5.
	ſiniſtrâ tenens
holding his Pollet, 6.	*Orbem Pictorium*, 6.
in his left-hand,	in quo *Pigmenta*
on which are the paints	quæ terebantur
which the Boy 7.	à puero 7.
ground on a Marble,	in *marmore*.
The Carver,	*Sculptor*
and Statuary	& *Statuarius*,
carve Statues, 8.	exſculpunt *Statuas*, 8.
of Wood and Stone.	è Ligno & Lapide.
The Graver	*Cælator*
and the Cutter	& *Scalptor* inſculpit
grave ſhapes 10.	Æri (Ligno)
and Characters	aliiſque Metallis,
with a graving Cheſil 9.	*Figuras* 10.
in Wood, Braſs,	& *Characteres*,
and other Metals.	*Cœlo*. 9.

LXXIX.

Specularia.

Looking-glasses.

Looking-Glasses 1.	*Specula* 1.
are provided,	parantur,
that Men may see	ut homines
themselves;	intueantur seipsos,
Spectacles, 2.	*Perspicilla*, 2.
that he may see better,	ut acrius cernat,
who hath a weak	qui habet
sight.	Visum debilem.
Things a far off,	Per *Telescopium*, 3.
are seen in a	
perspective-Glass, 3.	videntur remota,
as things neer	
at hand;	ut proxima;
A Flea appeareth	
in a multiplying glass	in *Microscopio*, 4.
like a little Hog. (4.	Pulex apparet
The rayes of the	ut Porcellus.
Sun, burn Wood	Radii Solis
thorow a burning-	accendunt ligna
glass, 5.	per *Vitrum urens*, 5.

LXXX.

Vietor:

The Cooper.

The

The Cooper, 1.
having an Apron 2.
tied about him,
maketh Hoops
of Hassel-rods, 3. (4.
upon a cutting-block,
with a Spoke-Shave, 5.
and Lags 6.
of Timber.

He maketh
Hogs-heads 7.
and Pipes, 8.
with two heads,
and Tubs, 9.
Soes, 10.
Flaskets, 11.
Buckets, 12.
with one Bottom,
of Lags.

Then he bindeth
them with Hoops, 13.
which he tyeth fast
with small Twigs, 15.
by means of
a Cramp Iron, 14.
and he fitteth them on
with a Mallet 16.
and a Driver. 17.

Vietor, 1.
amictus
Præcinctorio, 2.
facit
è *Virgis colurnis*, 3. (4.
super *Sellam incisoriam*
Scalpro bimanubriato,
Circulos, (5.
& ex *ligno*
Assulas. 6.

Ex *assulis*
conficit *Dolia* 7.
& *Cupas*, 8.
Fundo bino;
tum *Lacûs*, 9.
Labra, 10.
Pitynas 11.
& *Situlas*, 12.
fundo uno.

Postea vincit
Circulis, 13.
quos ligat
ope *Falcis vietoriæ*, 14.

Viminibus, 15.
& aptat
Tudite 16.
ac *Trudicula*. 17.

LXXXI.

Restio, & Lorarius.

The Roper, and the Cordwainer.

The Roper 1.	*Restio* 1.
twisteth	contorquet
Cords, 2.	*Funes* 2.
of Tow, or Hemp, 4.	agitatione
(which he wrappeth	*Rotulæ*, 3.
about himself)	è *Stupâ*, 4.
by the turning	vel *Cannabi*,
of a Wheel. 3.	quam sibi circumdat.
Thus there are	Sic fiunt,
made, first Cords, 5.	primò *Funiculi*, 5.
then Ropes, 6.	tum *Restes* 6.
and at last Cables. 7.	tandem *Rudentes*. 7.
The Cordwainer 8.	*Lorarius* 8.
cutteth great	scindit
Thongs, 10.	de *corio bubulo*, 9.
Bridles, 11.	*Loramenta*, 10.
Girdles, 12.	*Frena*, 11.
Sword-Belts, 13.	*Cingula*, 12.
Pouches, 14.	*Baltheos*, 13.
Port-mantles, 15. &c.	*Crumenas*, 14.
out of a Beast-hide. 9.	*Hippopéras*, 15. &c.

LXXXII.

The Traveller. *Viator.*

A Traveller 1.	*Viator*, 1.
beareth on his shoulders in a Budget, 2.	portat Humeris in *Bulga*, 2.
those things which his Satchel 3.	quæ non capit *Funda* 3.
or Pouch, 4.	vel *Marsupium*. 4.
cannot hold.	
He is covered with a Cloak ; 5.	Tegitur *Lacernâ* ; 5.
He holdeth a Staff 6.	Manu tenet *Baculum*, 6.
in his Hand, wherewith to bear up himself ;	quo se fulciat ;

He

He hath need of Provision for the way, as also of a pleasant Companion. 7.	Opus habet *Viatico*, ut & fido & facundo *Comite*. 7.
Let him not forsake the High-road, 9. for a Foot-way, 8. unless it be a beaten-Path.	Propter *Semitam*, 8. nisi sit *Callis tritus*, non deserat *Viam Regiam*. 9.
By-waies, 10. and places where two wayes meet 11. deceive, and lead men aside into uneven-places; 12. so do not by-paths, 13. and crosse-waies, 14.	*Avia*, 10. & *Bivia* 11, fallunt, & seducunt in *Salebras*; 12. non æquè, *Tramites* 13. & *Compita*. 14.
Let him therefore enquire of those he meeteth, 15. which way he must go; and let him take heed of Robbers, 16. as in the way, so also in the Inne, 17. where he lodgeth all Night.	Sciscitet igitur *Obvios*, 15. quà sit eundum; & caveat *Prædones*, 16. ut in viâ, sic etiam in *Diversorio*, 17. ubi pernoctat.

LXXXIII.

The Horſe-man. *Eques.*

The Horſe-man 1.	*Eques* 1.
ſetteth a Saddle, 3.	imponit *Equo* 2.
on his Horſe, 2.	*Ephippium*, 3.
and girdeth it on	idque ſuccingit
with a Girth ; 4	*Cingulo* ; 4.
He layeth	Inſternit etiam
a Saddle-Cloth 5.	*Dorſuale* ; 5.
alſo upon him;	
He decketh him	Ornat eum
with Trappings,	*Phaleris*,
a Fore-ſtall , 6.	*Frontali*, 6.
a Breaſt-Cloth, 7.	*Antilenâ*, 7.

and

and a Crupper. 8.	& *Postilenâ.* 8.
Then he getteth	Deinde
upon his Horse,	insilit in equum
putteth his Feet	indit pedes
into the Stirrops, 9.	*Stapedibus*, 9.
taketh the Bridle-rein, 10, 11.	sinistrâ capessit *Lorum* (habenam) 10. *Freni*, 11.
in his left-hand	
wherewith he guideth	quo equum
& holdeth the Horse;	flectit & retinet;
Then he putteth to	Tum
his Spurs, 12.	admovet *Calcaria*, 12.
and setteth him on	incitatque
with a Switch, 13.	*Virgulâ* 13.
and holdeth him in	& coërcet
with a Musrol. 14.	*Postomide*. 14.
The Holsters, 15.	*Bulgæ*,
hang down from the	pendent
Pummel of the	ex *apice*
Saddle, 16.	*ephippii*, 16.
in which the Pistols	quibus inseruntur
are put. 17.	*Sclopi*. 17.
The Rider is clad	Ipse eques induitur
in a short-Coat, 18,	*Chlamyde*; 18.
his Cloak being tyed	*Lacernâ* a tergo
behind him. 19.	revinctâ. 19.
A post 20.	*Veredarius* 20.
is carried on Horse-back a full Gallop.	cursim equo fertur.

Carriages.

LXXXIV.

Carriages. *Vehicula.*

We are carried
on a Sled 1.
over Snow,
and Ice.
A Carriage with one
Wheel, is called
a Wheel-barrow ; 2.
with two Wheels ,
a Cart ; 3.
with four Wheels,

Trahâ 1.
vehimur
ſuper nivibus
& Glacie.
Vehiculum unirotum,
dicitur
Pabo ; 2.
birotum,
Carrus ; 3.
quadrirotum,

a Wa-

a Wagon,	*Currus,*
which is either	qui
a Timber-Wagon, 4.	vel *Sarrácum,* 4.
or a Load-Wagon. 5.	vel *Plaustrum.* 5.
The parts of a Wa-	
gon are, the Neep,	Partes Currûs sunt,
(or draught-tree,) 6.	*Temo,* 6.
the Beam, 7.	*Jugum,* 7.
the Bottom, 8.	*Compages,* 8.
and the sides; 9. (10.	*Sponda;* 9.
Then the Axle-trees,	Tum *Axes,* 10.
about which the	circa quos currunt
Wheels run,	*Rotæ,* præfixis
the Lin-pins 11.	*Paxillis* 11.
and Axletree-staves, 12.	& *Obicibus.* 12.
being fastened before	
them.	
The Nave, 13.	Basis *Rotæ* 13.
is the ground-fast	est *Modiolus,* 14.
of the Wheel, 14.	ex quo prodeunt
from which come	duodecim *Radii;* 15.
twelve Spokes; 15.	Hos ambit
The Ring encom-	*Orbile,* compositum
passeth these, which is	è sex *Absidibus* 16.
made of six fellows 16.	& totidem *Canthis.* 17.
and as many Strakes. 17.	Currui
Hampiers, & Hurdles 18.	imponuntur
are set in	*Corbes* & *Crates.* 18.
a Wagon.	

Carrying

with a whip, 7.	*Scuticâ*, 7.
and guideth them	& flectit
with a String. 8.	*Funibus*. 8.
He greaseth the Axle-	Axem
tree with Axle-tree-	ungit
grease out of a grease-	ex *vase unguentario* 9.
pot 9.	
and stoppeth the wheel	*Axungiâ*;
with a trigen 10.	& inhibet rotam
in a steep descent.	*Sufflamine*, 10.
And thus the Coach	in præcipiti descensu
is driven along the	Et sic aurigatur
wheel-ruts. 11.	per *Orbitas*. 11.
Great persons are	*Magnates*
carryed with	vehuntur
six Horses 12.	*Sejugibus* 12.
by two Coach men,	duobus *Rhedariis*,
in a hanging-wagon,	Curru pensili
which is called	qui vocatur (13.
a Coach; 13.	*Carpentum* [pilentum;]
Others with two	Alii, *Bijugibus*, 14.
Horses, 14.	*Essedo*. 15.
in a Chariot 15.	*Arcera* 16.
Horse-Litters 16, 17.	& *Lecticæ* 17.
are carried by two	portantur
Horses.	à duobus equis.
They use Pack-hor-	Per invios montes
ses instead of Wagons	utuntur,
thorough Hills that are	loco Curruum,
not passable.	*jumentis Clitellariis*. 18.

Transitus

LXXXV.

Carrying to and fro. *Vectura.*

The Coach-man, 1.
joyneth a Horse fit to
match a Sadle-horse, 2, 3
to the Coach-tree,
with Thongs
or Chains 5.
hanging down from
the Collar 4.

Then he sitteth upon the Saddle-Horse,
and driveth those that
go before him 6.

Auriga, 1.
jungit
Parippum 2.
Sellario, 3.
ad *Temonem*,
de *Helcio* 4.
dependentibus
Loris vel *Catenis*. 5.

Deinde
insidet *Sellario*,
agit ante se
Antecessores 6.

with

LXXXVI.

Transitus aquarum.

Passing over waters.

Lest he that is to passe over a River should be all wet, Bridges 1. were invented for Carriages, and Foot-bridges 2. for Foot-men.	Trajecturus flumen ne madefiat, excogitati sunt *Pontes* 1. pro Vehiculis, & *Ponticuli* 2. pro Peditibus.
If a River have a Foord, 3. it is waded over. 4.	Si flumen habet *Vadum*, 3. vadatur. 4.
Flotes, 5. also are made of Timber pinned together; or Ferrie-boats, 6. of planks laid close together, for fear they should receive water.	Struuntur etiam *Rates*, 5 ex compactis tignis; vel *Pontones*, 6. ex trabibus consolidatis, ne aquam excipiant.
Besides Scullers 7. are made, which are rowed with an Oar, 8. or a Pole, 9. or haled with a haling-rope. 10.	Porrò fabricantur *Lintres* (Lembi) 7. qui aguntur *Remo*, 8. vel *Conto*, 9. aut trahuntur *Remulco*. 10.

LXXXVII.

Natatus.

Swimming.

Men

Men are wont also to swim over waters upon a bundle of flags, 1 & besides upon blown Beast-bladders ; 2. and after, by throwing their Hands & Feet 3. abroad.

Solent etiam tranare aquas, super *scirpeum fascem*, 1. porrò super inflatas *boum Vesicas* ; 2. deinde, liberè *jactatu manuum pedumque.* 3.

At last they learned to tread the water, 4. being plunged up to the girdle-stead, and carrying their Cloathes upon their Head.

Tandem didicerunt *calcare aquam*, 4. cingulo tenus immersi, & vestes supra caput gestando.

A Diver, 5. can swim also under the water, like a Fish.

Urinator, 5. etiam natare potest sub aquâ, ut Piscis.

LXXXVIII.

Navis actuaria.

A Galley.

A Ship furniſhed	*Navis* inſtructa
with Oars 1.	remis 1.
is a Barge 2.	eſt *Uniremis* 2.
or a Foyſt, &c.	vel *Biremis*, &c.
in which the	in quâ
Rowers, 3.	*Remiges*, 3.
ſitting	conſidentes
on Seats 4.	per *Tranſtra* 4.
by the Oar-Rings,	ad *Scalmos*,
Row 5.	aquam
by ſtriking the water	*Remis* pellendo,
with the Oars.	remigant. 5.
The Ship-Maſter 6.	*Proréta*, 6.
ſtanding in the	ſtans
Fore-Caſtel,	in *Prora*,
and the Steers-man 7.	& *Gubernator* 7.
ſitting at the Stern	ſedens in *Puppi*,
and holding the	tenensque
Rudder, 8.	*Clavum*, 8.
ſteer the Veſſel.	gubernant *Navigium*.

LXXXIX.

A Merchants-ſhip. *Navis oneraria.*

A Ship 1.
is driven onward, not
by Oars, but by the
only force of the
winds.
In it is a Maſt 2.
ſet up, faſtened
with Shrowds 3.
on all ſides to the
main-chains,
to which the
Sail-yards 4. (5.
are tyed, and the Sayls,
to theſe; which are

Navigium 1.
impellitur,
non remis,
ſed ſola vi ventorum.

In illo erigitur *Ma-*
undique (*lus*, 2.
ad *Oras Navis*
funibus 3. firmatus;

cui annectuntur
Antennæ, 4.
his, *Vela*, 5.
quæ ad Ventum

ſpread

spred open 6.	expanduntur 6.
to the wind, and are	& *Versoriis* 7.
hoysed by bowlings 7.	versantur.
The Sayls are	Vela sunt,
the main-Sayl, 8.	*Artemon*, 8.
the Trinket	
or fore-Sayl, 9.	*Dolon*, 9.
the Misen-Sayl,	
or Poop-Sayl. 10.	& *Epidromus*. 10. (11.
The Beak 11.	In *Prorâ* est *Rostrum*.
is in the fore-deck.	In *Puppi*,
The Ancient 12.	*Signum* (vexillum) 12.
placed in the Stern.	ponitur.
On the Mast	In malo
is the fore-top 13.	est *Corbis* 13.
the watch-tower of the	Navis *Specula*,
Ship, & over the fore-	& supra *galeam*
top a Vane 14.	*Aplustre* 14.
to shew which way the wind standeth.	Ventorum Index.
The Ship is stayed	*Anchorâ*, 15.
with an Anchor, 15.	navis sistitur.
The depth is	*Bolide*, 16.
fathomed with a	profunditas exploratur.
Plumet. 16.	
Passengers walk up	Navigantes
and down the Decks, 17.	deambulant
	in *Tabulato*. 17
The Sea-men run	Nautæ
to and fro through the	cursitant
Hatches. 18.	per *Foros*. 18.
And thus, even Seas	Atq; ita, etiam Maria
are passed over.	trajiciuntur. *Nau-*

XC.

Naufragium.

Ship-wrack.

When

When a Storm 1.	Cum *Procella* 1.
ariseth on a suddain,	repentè oritur,
they strike Sayl, 2.	contrahunt *Vela*, 2.
lest the Ship should be	ne Navis
dashed against Rocks 3.	ad *Scopulos* 3. allidatur,
or light upon	aut in *Brevia*(Syrtes)4.
shelves 4.	incidat.
If they cannot hinder her, they suffer	Si non possunt prohibere,
ship-wrack. 5.	patiuntur *Naufragium*. 5.
And then the Men, the wares, & all things are miserably lost.	Tum miserabiliter pereunt, Homines, *Merces*, omnia; (juvat
Nor doth the sheat-anchor, 6.	Neq; hîc quidquam *Sacra anchora*, 6.
being cast with a Cable, do any good.	*Rudenti* jacta.
Some escape,	Quidam evadunt,
either on a Plank 7.	vel *tabulâ* 7.
and by swimming,	ac enatando,
or in the Boat. 8.	vel *Scaphâ*. 8.
Part of the wares	Pars Mercium
with the dead Folks	cum mortuis
is carried out of the Sea 9.	a *Mari* 9.
upon the shoars.	in littora defertur,

Writing

XCI.

Writing. *Ars Scriptoria.*

The Ancients writ in Tables	Veteres ſcribebant
done over with wax	in *tabellis ceratis*
with a braſan poitrel, 1	æneo *Stilo*, 1.
with the ſharp end 2.	cujus parte cuſpidatâ 2.
whereof Letters were engraven, and rubbed out again with the broad end 3.	exarabantur literæ, planâ 3. verò rurſum obliterabantur.
Afterwards they writ Letters with a ſmall Reed. 4.	Deinde *literas* pingebant *ſubtili Calamo*. 4.
We uſe a Gooſe-quill, 5.	Nos utimur *anſerinâ Pennâ*, 5.

the

the Stem 6.	cujus *Caulem* 6.
of which we make	temperamus
with a Pen-knife; 7.	*Scalpello*, 7.
then we dip the neb	tum intingimus *Crenam*
in an Ink-horn, 8.	in *Atramentario*, 8.
which is stopped	quod obstruitur
with a stopple, 9.	*Operculo*, 9.
and we put up our Pens	& *Pennas* recondimus
into a Pennar. 10.	in *Calamario*. 10.
We dry a writing	Scripturam siccamus
with Blotting-paper.	*Chartâ bibula*,
or Calis-sand,	vel *arenâ scriptoriâ*,
out of a Sand-box. 11.	ex *Thecâ pulveraria*. 11.
And we indeed,	Et nos quidem,
write from the	scribimus
left-hand,	à sinistrâ
towards the right; 12.	dextrorsum; 12.
the Hebrews from	Hebræi
the right-hand	à dextrâ
towards the left; 13.	sinistrorsum; 13.
the Chinois,	Chinenses
and other Indians,	& Indi alii,
from the top down-wards. 14.	à summo deorsum. 14.

XCII.

Papyrus.

Paper.

The ancients used	Veteres utebantur
Beech-Bords, 1.	*Tabulis faginis*, 1.
or Leaves 2.	aut *Foliis* 2.
as also Barks 3.	ut & *Libris* 3.
of Trees,	*Arborum*, præsertim
especially of an Egyptian shrub,	arbusculæ Ægyptiæ,
which was called	cui nomen erat
Papyrus.	*Papyrus*.
Now Paper is in use,	Nunc, est in usu
which the Paper-	*Charta*,
maker maketh in	quam *Chartopæus*,
a Paper-mill, 4.	in *molâ papyraceâ*, 4.
of Linnen-rags, 5.	conficit è *linteis vetu-*
stamped to Mash, 6.	in *pulmentum* (*stis*, 5.
which being taken	contusis, 6.
up in Frames, 7.	quod, *Normulis*
he spreadeth into	haustum, 7.
Sheets, 8.	diducit
and setteth them in	in *Plagulas*, 8.
the air that they may	aerique exponit,
be dried.	ut siccentur.
Twenty five of	Harum XXV.
these make a quire, 9.	faciunt *Scapum*, 9.
twenty quires	XX. Scapi
a Ream, 10.	*Volumen minus*, 10.
and ten of these	horum X.
a Bale of paper. 11.	*Volumen majus*. 11.
That which is to last	Diu duraturum,
long is written in	scribitur in
Parchment. 12.	*Membrana*. 12.

Printing

XCIII.

Printing | *Typographia.*

The Printer
hath Copper Letters
in a great number
put into Boxes. 5.
The Compositor 1.
taketh them out
one by one, and
(according to
the Copy,
which he hath fastened
before him in a
Visorum 2.)
composeth words

Typographus
habet *æneos Typos*,
magno numero,
diſtributos
per *Loculamenta*. 5.
Typotheta 1.
eximit illos
ſingulatim,
& componit
(ſecundum *Exemplar*,
quod *Retinaculo* 2.
ſibi præfixum habet)
verba

in a compoſing-ſtick, 3.
till a Line be made,
he putteth theſe in
a Galley, 4.
till a Page 6.
be made, and theſe
again in a Form, 7.
and he locketh them up
in Iron Chaſes, 8.
with coyns, 9.
leſt they ſhould
drop out, and putteth
them under the
Preſs. 10.

Then the Preſs-man
beateth it over with
Printers-ink by means
of Balls, 11.
ſpreadeth upon it the
Papers,
put in the Frisket, 12.
which being put under
the Spindle, 14.
on the Coffin, 13.
and preſſed down
with the Bar 15.
he maketh to take
Impreſſion.

Gnomone, 3.
donec fiat *Verſus*;
hos indit
Forma, 4.
donec fiat *Pagina*; 6.
has iterum
tabula compoſitoria, 7.
eoſque coarctat
Marginibus ferreis, 8.
ope *Coclearum*, 9.
ne dilabantur;
ac ſubjicit
Prælo. 10.

Tum *Impreſſor*,
ope *Pilarum*, 11.
illinit
Atramento impreſſorio:
ſuperimponit,
inditas *Operculo* 12.
Chartas,
quas,
in *Tigello* 13.
ſubditas
Trochlea, 14.
& *Sucula* 15.
impreſſas,
facit
typos imbibere.

Biblio-

XCIV.

Bibliopolium.

The Book-ſellars Shop.

The

The Book-seller 1.	*Bibliopóla* 1.
selleth Books	vendit Libros
in a Booksellars-shop, 2	in *Bibliopolio*, 2.
of which he writeth a Catalogue. 3.	quorum conscribit *Catalogum*. 3.
The Books are	Libri disponuntur
placed on Shelves, 4.	per *Repositoria*, 4.
and are laid open	& ad usum,
for use upon a Desk 5.	super *Pluteum* 5. exponuntur
A Multitude of Books	Multitudo Librorum,
is called	vocatur
a Library. 6.	*Bibliotheca*. 6.

XCV.

Bibliopegus.

The Book-binder.

In

In times past	Olim
they glued Paper	agglutinabant
to Paper, and rolled	Chartam chartæ,
them up together into	convolvebantque eas
one Rowl. 1.	in unum *Volumen*. 1.
At this day	Hodiè
the Bookbinder	compingit Libros
bindeth Books,	*Compactor*,
whilst he wipeth 2.	dum Chartas
over Papers	*aquâ glutinosâ*
steept in Gum-water;	maceratas, terget; 2.
and then foldeth	
them together, 3.	deinde complicat, 3.
beateth with a	malleat, 4.
hammer, 4. up, 5	tum consuit, 5.
then stitcheth them	
presseth them	comprimit
in a Press, 6.	*Prelo*, 6.
which hath two	(quod habet
Scrues 7. (back,	duas *Cochleas* 7.)
glueth them on the	dorso conglutinat,
cutteth off the edges	rotundo *Cultro* 8.
with a round Knife, 8.	demarginat,
and at last covereth	tandem
them with Parchment	*Membranâ*
or Leather, 9	vel *Corio* 9.
maketh them hand-	vestit, efformat,
some, and setteth on	& affigit
Clasps. 10.	*Uncinulos*. 10.

XCVI.

Liber.

A Book.

A Book,	Liber,
as to its outward	quoad formam
ſhape is either	exteriorem,
in Folio, 1.	eſt vel in *Folio*, 1.
or in Quarto, 2.	vel in *Quarto*, 2.
in Octavo, 3.	in *Octavo*, 3.
in Duodecimo, 4.	in *Duodecimo*, 4.
either made to open	
Side-wiſe, 5.	vel *Columnatus*, 5.
or Long wiſe, 6.	vel *Linguatus*, 6.
with Brazen Claſps, 7.	cum *Clauſuris aeneis*, 7.
or Strings, 8	vel *Ligulis*, 8.
and Square-boſſes. 9.	& *Bullis angularibus*. 9.
Within are	Intùs
Leaves 10	ſunt *Folia* 10.
with two Pages,	duabus *Paginis*.
ſometimes divided	aliquando
with Columns 11.	*Columnis* diviſa, 11.
	cumque
and Marginal Notes.12	*notis marginalibus*. 12.

XCVII.

Schola.

A School.

A School 1.
is a Shop, in which
Young Wits
are fashion'd to Vertue,
and it is distinguished
into Forms.

The Master, 2.
sitteth in a Chair; 3.
the Scholars, 4.
in Forms; 5.
he teacheth,
they learn.

Some things
are writ down before
them with Chalk
on a Table. 6.

Some
sit at a Table,
and write : 7.
he mendeth 8.
their Faults.

Some stand and
rehearse things com-
mitted to memory. 9.

Some talk
together, 10.
& behave themselves
wantonly,
and carelesly ;
these are chastised
with a Ferula 11.
and a Rod. 12.

Schola 1.
est officina, in quâ
novelli animi
ad virtutem formantur,
& distinguitur
in *Classes.*

Præceptor, 2.
sedet in *Cathedrâ* ; 3.
Discipuli, 4.
in *Subselliis* ; 5.
ille docet,
hi discunt.

Quædam
præscribuntur illis
cretâ
in *tabellâ.* 6.

Quidam
sedent ad mensam,
& scribunt : 7.
ipse corrigit 8.
Mendas.

Quidam stant,
& recitant
memoriæ mandata. 9.

Quidam confabu-
lantur, 10.
ac gerunt se
petulantes
& negligentes :
hi castigantur
Ferulâ (baculo) 11.
& *Virgâ.* 12.

XCVIII.

The Study. *Muséum.*

The Study 1.
is a place
where a Student, 2.
a part from men,
sitteth alone,
addicted to his Studies,
whilst he readeth
Books, 3.
which being within
his reach, he layeth
open upon a Desk 4.
and picketh all the
best things out of
them into his own
Manual, 5.

Muséum 1.
est locus,
ubi studiosus, 2.
secretus ab hominibus,
solus sedet,
Studiis deditus,
dum lectitat
Libros, 3.
quos penes se
super *Pluteum* 4.
exponit, & ex illis
in *Manuale* 5. suum
optima quæq; excerpit,
or

or marketh them in them with a dash, 6.	aut in illis *Liturâ*, 6.
or a little star, 7. in the Margent.	vel ad *marginem* *Asterisco*, 7. notat.
Being to sit up late, he setteth a Candle, 8.	Lucubraturus, elevat *Lychnum* (*candelam*) 8.
on a Candle-stick, 9.	in *Candelabro*, 9.
which is snuffed with Snuffers; 10.	qui emungitur *Emunctorio*; 10.
before the Candle he placeth a Screen, 11.	ante Lychnum collocat *Umbraculum*, 11.
which is green, that it may not hurt his eye-sight; richer persons use a Taper,	quod viride est, ne hebetet oculorum aciem: opulentiores utuntur *Cereo*,
for a Tallow-Candle stinketh, and smoaketh.	nam *Candela sebacea* fœtet & fumigat.
A Letter 12. is wrapped up, writ upon, 13. and sealed. 14.	*Epistola* 12. complicatur, inscribitur, 13. & obsignatur. 14.
Going abroad by night, he maketh use of a Lanthorn 15. or a Torch. 16.	Noctu prodiens, utitur *Laternâ* 15. vel *Face*.

Artes

XCIX.

Arts belonging to the *Speech*.	*Artes Sermonis.*

Grammar, 1.	*Grammatica* 1.
is conversant	versatur
about Letters, 2.	circa *Literas*, 2.
of which it maketh	ex quibus componit
words 3.	*Voces* (*verba* 3.
& teacheth how to utter,	easq; docet rectè eloqui
write, 4.	scribere, 4.
put together,	construere,
and part them rightly.	distinguere [interpun-
Rhetorick, 5.	*Rhetorica* 5. (gere.]
doth as it were	
paint 6.	pingit 6. quasi
a rude Form 7.	rudem *formam* 7.
of Speech with Oratory	Sermonis *Oratoriis*

Flor

Flouriſhes, 8.	*pigmentis*, 8.
ſuch as are, Figures,	ut ſunt, *Figuræ*,
Elegancies,	*Elegantiæ*,
Adagies,	*Adagia* (proverbia)
Apophthegms,	*Apophthegmata*,
Sentences,	*Sententiæ* (Gnomæ)
Similies,	*Similia*
Hieroglyphicks, *&c.*	*Hieroglyphica*, &c.
Poetry 9.	*Poeſis* 9.
gathereth theſe Flours of Speech 10.	colligit hos *Flores Orationis* 10.
& tyeth them as it were into a little Garland, 11.	& colligat quaſi in *Corollam*, 11.
and ſo making of Proſe a Poem,	atque ita, faciens e *proſâ ligatam orationem*,
it maketh ſeveral ſorts of Verſes,	componit varia *Carmina*,
and Odes,	& *Hymnos* (*Odas*)
and is therefore crown'd with a Laurel. 12.	ac propterea coronatur *Lauru*. 12.
Muſique, 13.	*Muſica*, 13.
ſetteth Tunes, 14.	componit *Notis* *Melodias*, 14.
with Pricks, to which it fitteth words	quibus Verba aptat,
and ſo ſingeth alone,	atque ita cantat ſola
or in Conſort,	vel *Concentu* (*Symphoniâ*)
or by voyce,	aut voce,
or Muſical Inſtrument. 15.	aut inſtrumentis Muſicis. 15.

Muſical

C.

Musical Instruments. *Instrumenta Musica.*

Musical Instruments are
those which make a
First, (sound:
when they are beaten
as a Cymbal 1. (upon
with a Pestil,
a little Bell, 2.
with an Iron Pellet
a Rattle, 3. (within;
by tossing it about;
a Jews-Trump, 4.
being put to the mouth,
with the finger;
a Drum 5.
and a Kettle, 6.

Musica Instrumenta sunt
quæ edunt vocem:
Primò,
cùm pulsantur,
ut *Cymbalum* 1.
Pistillo,
Tintinnabulum 2.
intus *Globulo ferreo;*
Crepitaculum, 3.
circumversando;
Crembalum, 4.
ori admotum,
digito;
Tympanum 5.
& *Ahenum,* 6.

with

with a *Drum-stick*, 7.	*Claviculâ*, 7.
as also the Dulcimer, 8.	ut & *Sambuca*, 8.
with the shepherds-harp; 9.	cum *Organo pastoritio* ; 9.
and the Tymbrel. 10.	& *Sistrum* (Crotalum.) 10.
Secondly,	Secundò,
upon which strings are	in quibus *Chordæ*
stretched, and struck upon,	intenduntur & plectuntur,
as the Psalterie, 11.	ut *Nablium*, 11.
and the Virginals, 12.	cum *Clavicordio*, 12.
with both hands;	utrâque manu ;
	Dexterâ tantùm,
the Lute 13.	*Testudo* (Chelys) 13.
in which is the Neck, 14.	(in quâ *Jugum*, 14.
the Belly, 15.	*Magadium*, 15.
the Pegs, 16.	& *Verticilli*, 16.
by which the Strings, 17.	quibus *Nervi* 17.
are stretched upon	intenduntur
the Bridge, 18.	super *Ponticulam* 18.)
the Cittern; 19.	& *Cythara* ; 19.
with the right hand only,	*Pandura*, 20.
the Vial, 20.	*Plectro*; 21.
with a Bow; 21.	& *Lyra*, 23.
and the Harp, 23.	intùs rotâ,
with a wheel within,	quæ versatur :
which is turned about,	In singulis,
the Stops, 22.	*Dimensiones* 22.
in every one are touched	sinistrâ tanguntur.
with the left hand.	Tandem
At last,	quæ inflantur,
those which are blown,	ut, Ore,
as with the mouth,	*Fistula* (*Tibia*) 24.
the Flute, 24.	*Gingras*, 25.
the Shawm, 25.	*Tibia utricularis*, 26.
the Bag-pipe, 26.	*Lituus*, 27.
the Corner, 27.	*Tuba*, 28.
the Trumpet; 28 : 29.	*Buccina* ; 29.
or with bellows, as,	vel *Follibus* 30.
a pair of Organs : 30.	ut, *Organum pneumaticum*.

Philo-

CI.

Philosophia.

Philosophy.

The

The Naturalist, 1.	*Physicus*, 1.
vieweth all the	speculatur
works of God	omnia Dei Opera
in the World.	in Mundo.
The Supernaturalist, 2.	*Metaphysicus*, 2.
searcheth out the	perscrutatur
Causes, & Effects	rerum
of things.	*Causas* & *Effecta.*
The Arithmetician,	*Arithmeticus*,
reckoneth numbers,	computat numeros
by adding,	addendo,
substracting,	subtrahendo,
multiplying,	multiplicando,
and dividing;	dividendo;
and that either	
by Cyphers 3.	idque vel *Cyphris* 3.
on a slate,	in *Palimpsesto*,
or by Counters 4.	vel *Calculis* 4.
upon a Deck:	super *Abacum*:
Countrey-people	*Rustici*
reckon 5.	numerant 5.
with figures of tens X.	*Decussibus* X.
and Figures of five V.	& *Quincuncibus* V.
by twelves,	per *Duodenas*,
Fifteens,	*Quindenas*,
and threescorees	& *Sexagenas*.

CII.

Geometria.

Geometrie.

A Geometrician	*Geometra*
measureth	metitur
the heighth of	*altitudinem*
a Tower, 1. . . . 2.	*Turris*, 1. . . . 2.
or the distance	aut *distantiam*
of places, 3 . . . . 4.	*Locorum*, 3. . . . 4.
either with	sive *Quadrante*, 5.
a Quadrate, 5.	sive *Radio*. 6.
or a Jacobs-staff. 6.	
He marketh out the	*Figuras rerum*
Figures of things,	designat
with Lines, 7.	*Lineis*, 7.
Angles, 8.	*Angulis*, 8.
and Circles, 9.	& *Circulis*, 9.
by a Rule, 10.	ad *Regulam*, 10.
a Squire, 11. (ses 12.	*Normam* 11.
and a pair of Compas-	& *Circinum*. 12.
Out of these	Ex his
	oriuntur
arise an Oval, 13.	*Cylindrus*, 13.
a Triangle, 14.	*Trigonus*, 14.
a quadrangle 15.	*Tetragonus*, 15.
and other Figures.	& aliæ figuræ.

CIII.

The celeſtial Sphære. *Sphæra cœleſtis.*

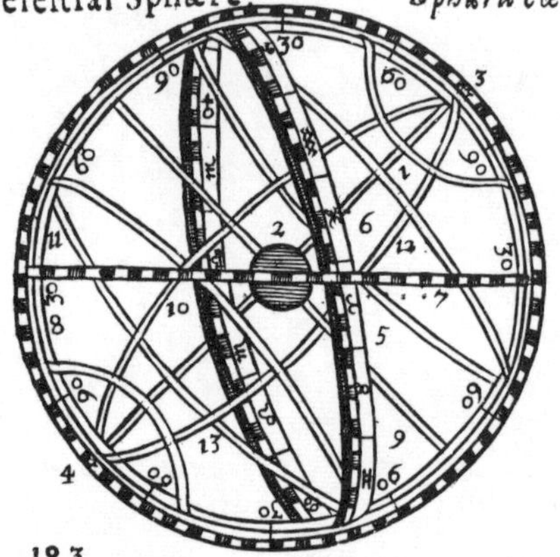

103

Aſtronomie conſidereth
the motion of the Stars,
Aſtrologie the effects
of them.

The Globe of Heaven
is turned about upon
an Axle-tree 1.
about the Globe of
the earth, 2.
in the ſpace of XXIV hours.

The polar ſtars, or Poles,
the Arctick 3.
and Antartick 4.
conclude the Axle-tree
at both ends.

The Heaven is full of
Stars every where.
There are reckoned above
a thouſand fixed-ſtars;
but of conſtellations

Aſtronomia conſiderat
Aſtrorum motus,
Aſtrologia
eorum effectûs.

Cœli Globus
volvitur
ſuper *Axem* 1.
circa *globum*
Terræ, 2.
ſpacio XXIV. horarum.

Axem utrinq; finiunt
Stellæ Polares ſive *Poli*,
Arcticus 3.
& *Antarcticus*. 4.

Cœlum
undique eſt ſtellatum:
Stellarum fixarum
numerantur plus *mille*;
Siderum verò

towards

towards the North, XXI
towards the South, XVI
And to these the XII. Signs
of the Zodiaque, 5.
every one of XXX degrees,
whose names are, ♈ Aries,
♉ Taurus, ♊ Gemini.
♋ Cancer, ♌ Leo, ♍ Virgo,
♎ Libra, ♏ Scorpius,
♐ Sagittarius, ♑ Capricor.
♒ Aquarius, ♓ Pisces.
Under this the seven
wandering Stars,
which they call Planets,
move, whose way is a circle
in the middle of the
Zodiack, called
the Ecliptick. 6.
Other circles are
the Horizon, 7.
the Meridian, 8.
the Æquator; 9.
the two Colures,
the one of the Æquinocts, 10
(of the Spring,
when the ☉ entreth into ♈
Autumnal,
when it entreth into ♎)
the other of the Solstices, 11
(of the Summer,
when the ☉ entreth into ♋
of the Winter
when it entreth into ♑)
the two Tropicks,
the Tropick of Cancer, 12.
the Tropick of Capricorn, (13.
and the two
polar circles. 14... 15.

Septentrionalium, XXI.
Meridionalium, XVI.
Adde *Signa* XII.
Zodiaci, 5
quodlibet graduum XXX.
quorum nomina sunt,
♈ *Aries*, ♉ *Taurus*, ♊ *Gemini*
♋ *Cancer*, ♌ *Leo*, ♍ *Virgo*,
♎ *Libra*, ♏ *Scorpius*.
♐ *Sagittarius* ♑ *Capricornus*,
♒ *Aquarius*, ♓ *Pisces*.
Sub hoc, cursitant
Stellæ errantes VII.
quas vocant *Planetas*,
quorum via est,
Circulus in medio Zodiaci,
dictus, *Ecliptica*. 6.
Alii Circuli sunt,
Horizon, 7.
Meridianus, 8.
Æquator; 9.
duo *Coluri*,
alter *Æquinoctiorum*, 10.
(*Verni*
quando ☉ ingreditur ♈
Autumnalis
quando ingreditur ♎)
alter *Solstitiorum*, 11.
(*Æstivi*
quando ☉ ingreditur ♋,
Hyberni
quando ingreditur ♑;)
duo *Tropici*,
Tr. *Cancri*, 12.
Tr. *Capricorni*; 13.
& duo *Polares*. 14... 15.

CIV.

Planetarum Adspectus.

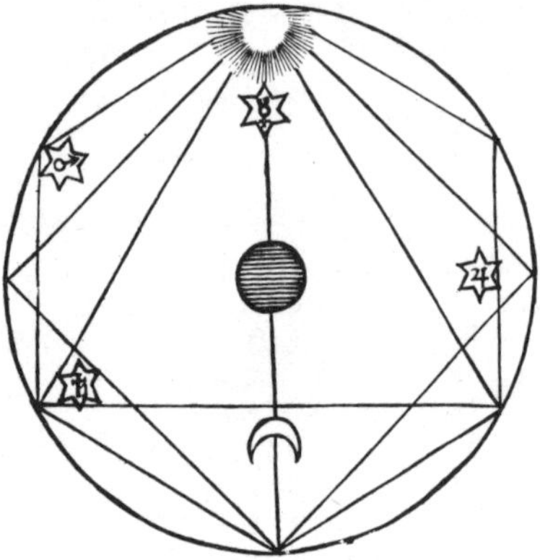

104

The Aspects of the Planets.

The

The Moon ☽	*Luna* ☽
runneth thorow the Zodiaque every Moneth.	percurrit *Zoadicam* singulis *Mensibus*.
The Sun, ☉	*Sol*, ☉
in a year;	Anno;
Mercury ☿	*Mercurius* ☿
and Venus, ♀	& *Venus*, ♀
about the Sun,	circa Solem,
the one in a hundred and fifteen, the other in 585. daies.	ille CXV, hæc DLXXXV. Diebus.
Mars, ♂	*Mars*, ♂
in two years;	Biennio;
Jupiter, ♃	*Jupiter*, ♃
in almost twelve;	ferè duodecim;
Saturn, ♄	*Saturnus*, ♄
in thirty years.	triginta annis.
Hereupon they meet variously amongst themselves, and have mutual aspects one towards another.	Hinc variè inter se conveniunt & se mutuò adspiciunt:
As here the ☉ and ☿ are in Conjunction,	Ut hîc, sunt ☉ & ☿ in *Conjunctione*,
☉ and ☽ in Opposition,	☉ & ☽ in *Oppositione*,
☉ and ♄ in Trine, Aspect,	☉ & ♄ in *Trigono*,
☉ and ♃ in a Quartile,	☉ & ♃ in *Quadraturâ*,
☉ and ♂ in a Sextile.	☉ & ♂ in *Sextili*.

CV.

Phases Lunæ.

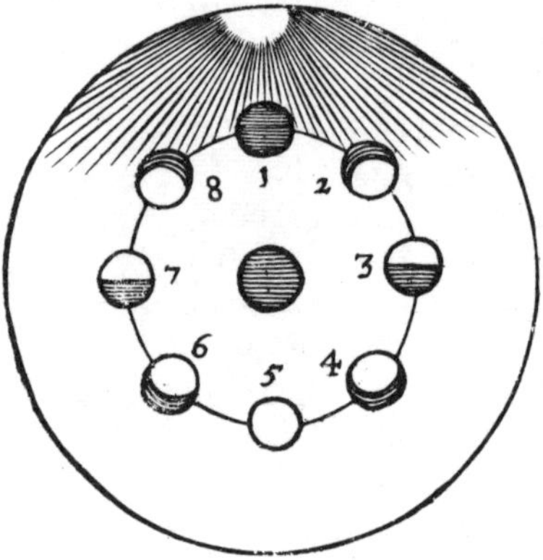

105

The Apparitions of the Moon.

The Moon,	*Luna*,
shineth not by her	lucet,
own Light,	non suâ propriâ.
but that which is	sed à *Sole* mutuatâ
borrowed of the Sun.	*Luce*.
For the one half	Nam,
of it is alwaies enlight-ned the other	altera ejus medietas semper illuminatur,
remaineth darkish.	altera manet caliginosa.
Hereupon we see it	Hinc videmus,
in Conjunction with the Sun, 1.	in *conjunctione Solis*, 1.
to be obscure, almost, none at all;	obscuram, imo nullam:
in Opposition, 5.	in *Oppositione*, 5.
whole and clear,	totam & lucidam
(and we call it the Full Moon ;)	(& vocamus *Plenilunium* :)
sometimes in the half,	alias dimidiam,
(and we call it the Prime 3. and last quarter ; 7.	(& dicimus *primam* 3. & *ultimam* 7. *Quadram*)
Otherwise	Cæteroqui
it wareth 2 ....4.	crescit 2....4.
or waneth 6....8.	aut decrescit, 6...8.
and is said to be	& vocatur
horned or more than half round.	*Falcata* vel *gibbosa*.

CVI.

Eclipses.

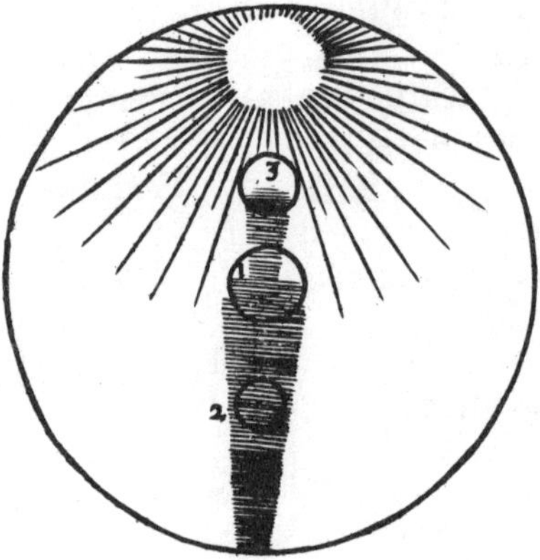

106

The Eclipses.

The

The Sun
is the fountain of light,
inlightning all things;
but the Earth, 1.
and the Moon, 2.
being shady Bodies,
are not pierced
with its Rayes,
for they cast a shadow
upon the place just
over against them.
Therefore,
when the Moon lighteth
into the shadow of the
it is darkned (Earth 2.
which we call
an Eclipse, or defect.
But when
the Moon runneth
betwixt the Sun
and the Earth 3.
it covereth it
with its shadow:
and this we call
the Eclipse of the Sun,
because it taketh from
us the sight of the sun,
and its light;
neither doth the Sun
for all that suffer any
thing, but the Earth.

Sol,
est fons Lucis,
illuminans omnia:
sed non penetrantur
Radiis ejus
Corpora opaca,
Terra, 1.
& *Luna*; 2.
nam jaciunt umbram
in locum oppositum.

Ideò,
cum Luna incidit
in umbram Terræ, 2.
obscuratur:
quod vocamus
Eclipsin [deliquium]
Cum vero (*Luna*.
Luna currit
inter Solem
& Terram, 3.
obtegit illum
umbrâ suâ:
& hoc vocamus
Eclipsin Solis,
quia nobis adimit
prospectum Solis
& lucem ejus;
nec tamen Sol
aliquid patitur,
sed Terra.

The

CVII. 2.

The terrestrial Sphere. *Sphæra terrestris.*

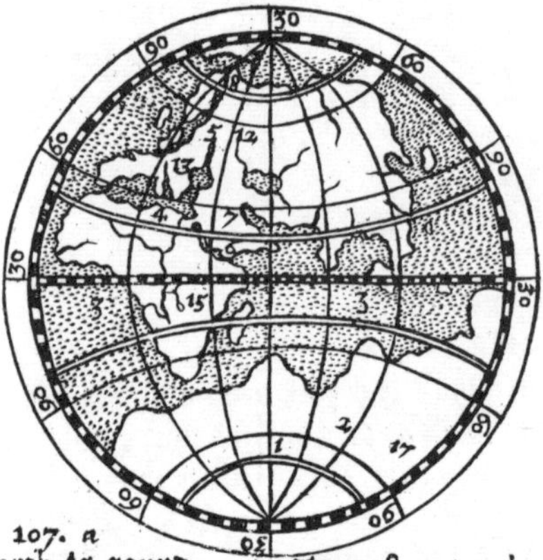

107. *a*

The Earth is round,	*Terra* est rotunda,
& therefore to be represented	fingenda igitur
by two Hemisphæres, a . . b	duobus *Hemisphæriis.* a . . b
The circuit of it (grees	Ambitus ejus,
is three hundred and sixty de-	est *graduum* CCCLX.
(whereof every one maketh	(quorum quisque facit
fifteen German miles)	Milliaria Germanica XV)
or 5400 miles ;	seu Milliarium VMCCCC :
and yet it is but a prick	& tamen est Punctum,
compared with the world	collata cum Orbe,
whereof it is the Centre.	cujus *Centrum* est.
They measure the longi-	Longitudinem ejus
tude of it by Climates,	demetiuntur *Climatibus*, 1.
and the Latitude	Latitudinem,
by parallels. 2. (it about,	lineis *Parallelis.* 2.
The Ocean 3. compasseth	Eam ambit *Oceanus*, 3.
and five Seas wash it	& perfundunt V *Maria*,
the Mediterrane Sea, 4.	*Mediterraneum*, 4.
the Baltick Sea, 5. the Red	*Balticum*, 5. *Erythræum*, 6.
Sea 6. the Persian Sea, 7.	*Persicum*, 7. *Caspium*. 8.
and the Caspian Sea, 8.	

CVII.b

The terrestrial Sphere. *Sphæra terrestris.*

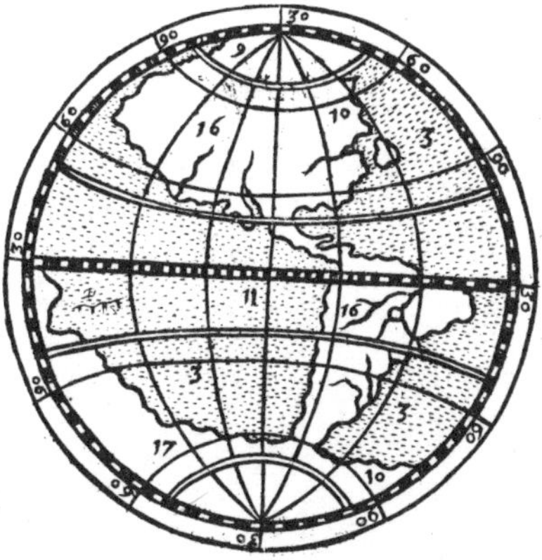

107.b

It is divided into 5 Zones,
whereof the 2 frigid ones 9.9
are inhabitable,
the 2 Temperate ones, 10...10
& the Torrid one, 11. habita-
Besides it is divided (ble
into three Continents;
this of ours, 12. which is
into Europe, 13. (subdivided
Asia, 14. Africa, 15.
America, 16... 16.
(whose inhabitants
are Antipodes to us)
and the South-land 17... 17.
yet unknown.
They that dwell under the
North-pole, 18. have the days
and nights 6 months long
Infinite Islands
float in the Seas.

Distribuitur in *Zonas* V.
quarum *duæ frigidæ*, 9 . . 9.
sunt inhabitabiles;
duæ *Temperatæ*, 10 . . . 10.
& *Torrida*, 11. habitantur.
Ceterum divisa est
in tres *Continentes*:
Nostram, 12. quæ subdividi-
in *Europam*, 13. (tur
Asiam, 14 & *Africam*, 15.
in *Americam*, 16 . . . 16.
cujus incolæ
nobis sunt *Antipodes*;
& in *Terram Australem*, 17...17
adhuc incognitam.
Habitantes sub *Arcto*, 18.
semestrales habent
Noctes Diesque.
In maribus,
Infinitæ natant *Insulæ*.

Europa.

CVIII.

Europa.

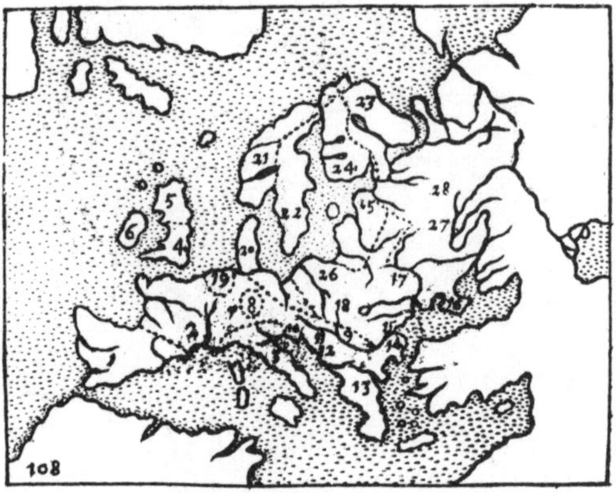

Europe.

The

The cheif Kingdoms in our Europe, are	In *Europâ* nostrâ, sunt *Regna* primaria,
Spain, 1	*Hispania*, 1.
France, 2.	*Gallia*, 2.
Italy, 3.	*Italia* 3.
England, 4.	*Anglia* (Britania) 4.
Scotland, 5.	*Scotia*, 5.
Ireland, 6.	*Hibernia*, 6.
Germany, 7.	*Germania* 7.
Bohemia, 8.	*Bohemia*, 8.
Hungary, 9.	*Hungaria*, 9.
Croatia, 10.	*Croatia*, 10.
Dacia, 11.	*Dacia* 11.
Sclavonia, 12.	*Sclavonia*, 12.
Greece, 13.	*Græcia*, 13.
Thrace, 14.	*Thracia*, 14.
Podolia, 15.	*Podolia*, 15.
Tartary, 16.	*Tartaria*, 16.
Lituania, 17.	*Lituania*, 17.
Poland, 18.	*Polonia*, 18.
The Netherlands, 19.	*Belgium*, 19.
Denmark, 20.	*Dania*, 20.
Norway, 21.	*Norvegia*, 21.
Swethland, 22.	*Suecia*, 22.
Lapland, 23.	*Lappia*, 23.
Finland, 24.	*Finnia*, 24.
Lifland, 25.	*Livonia*, 25.
Prussia, 26.	*Borussia*, 26.
Muscovy, 27.	*Moscovia*, 27.
and Russia, 28.	*Russia*, 28.

CIX.

Moral Philosophy. *Ethica.*

This Life is a way,
or a place divided into
two ways, like
Pythagoras's letter Y;
broad 1.
on the left-hand track,
narrow 2.
on the right;
that belongs to Vice 3.
this to Virtue, 4.
Mind, Young man, 5.
imitate Hercules.
leave the left-hand way,
turn from Vice.

Vita hæc, est *via*,
sive *Bivium*,
simile
Literæ *Pythagoricæ* Y;
sinistro tramite
latum 1.
dextro
angustum; 2.
ille *Vitii* 3. est,
hic *Virtutis* 4.
Adverte, juvenis, 5.
Herculem imitare.
Sinistram linque,
Vitium aversare:

the Entrance is fair,	speciosus *Aditus*,
but the End, 7.	sed turpis
is ugly & steep down.	& præceps *Exitus*. 7.
Go on the right hand,	Dexterâ ingredere,
though it be thorny, 8.	utut spinosâ: 8.
no way is	nulla via
unpassable to vertue;	invia Virtuti;
follow (eth	Sequere,
whither virtue lead-	quò ducit Virtus,
through narrow places	per *angusta*
to stately places,	ad *augusta*,
to the tower of honour,	ad *arcem honoris*, 9.
Keep the middle (9.	Medium tene
and straight path (safe.	& rectum *tramitem*;
and thou shalt go very	tutissimus ibis.
Take heed thou do	Cave excedas
not go too much on	ad dextram, 10.
the right hand: 10.	
Bridle in, 12.	Affectûs,
the wild horse, 11.	equum ferocem, 11.
of Affection, (headlong.	compesce freno, 12.
lest thou fall down.	ne præceps fias.
See thou dost not go	Cave deficias
amiss on the left-	ad Sinistram, 13.
hand, 13.	
in an Ass-like	segnitie asininâ: 14.
sluggishness, 14.	
but go onwards	sed progredere
constantly,	constanter,
persevere to the end,	pertende ad finem,
and thou shalt be	& coronaberis. 15.
crowned, 15.	

CX.

Prudence. *Prudentia.*

Prudence, 1.
looketh upon all things
as a Serpent, 2.
and doeth,
speaketh, or thinketh
nothing in vain.
She looks backward, 3
as into a lookingglass,
to things past; (4.
and seeth before her, 5.
as with a Perspective-glass, 7.
things to come,
or the end; 6.
and so she perceiveth,

Prudentia, 1.
omnia circumspectat
ut *Serpens*, 2.
nihilq; agit,
loquitur, & cogitat
incassum.
Respicit, 3
tanquam in *Speculum*, 4
& *prospicit*, 5.
ad *Præterita*;
tanquam *Telescopio*, 7.

Futura
seu *Finem*: 6.
atq; ita perspicit,

what

what she hath done,	quid egerit,
and what remaineth to	& quid agendum re-
be done.	stet.
She proposeth an	Actionibus suis
Honest,	præfigit *Scopum*,
Profitable, (done,	*Honestum*,
and withal, if it may be	*Utilem*,
a pleasant End	simúlque si fieri potest,
to her actions.	*Jucundum*.
Having foreseen	*Fine* prospecto,
the End,	dispicit
she looketh out Means,	*Media*,
as a Way, 8 (end;	ceu *Viam*, 8.
which leadeth to the	quæ ducit ad Finem;
but such as are certain	sed certa & facilia,
and easie, and fewer	pauciora potius
rather than more,	quam plura:
lest any thing should	ne quid impediat.
hinder. (tunity, 9.	
She watcheth Oppor-	*Occasioni* 9.
(which having	(quæ,
a bushy forehead, 10.	*Fronte Capillata*, 10.
& being bald-pated, 11.	sed Vertice *calva*, 11.
and moreover having	adhæc *alata*, 12.
wings, 12.	facilè elabitur)
doth quickly slip away)	attendit,
and catcheth it.	eamque captat.
She goeth	In viâ pergit
on her way warily,	cautè (providè)
for fear she should	ne impingat
stumble or go amiss,	aut aberret.

CXI.

Diligence. *Sedulitas.*

Diligence 1.
loveth labours,
avoideth Sloth,
is alwaies at work,
like the Pismire, 2.
and carrieth together,
as she doth, for her self,
store of all things. 3.
She doth not alwaies
sleep, or make holydays,

Sedulidas 1.
amat labores,
fugit *Ignaviam*,
semper est in *opere*.
ut *Formica*, 2.
& comportat sibi,
ut illa, *am*. 3.
omnium rerum *Copi-*
Non dormit semper
aut ferias agit,

as the Sluggard, 4.	ut *Ignavus* 4.
& the Grasshopper 5.	& *Cicada*; 5.
whom Want 6. (do;	quos tandem
at the last overtaketh.	premit *Inopia* 6.
She pursueth what	Incepta.
things she hath under-taken cheerfully,	urget alacriter,
even to the end;	ad finem usque;
she putteth nothing off till the morrow,	nihil procrastinat,
nor doth she sing	nec cantat
the Crows song, 7. (ver	cantilenam *Corvi*, 7.
which saith over and o-	qui ingeminat
Cras, Cras.	*Cras*, *Cras*.
After labours under-	Post *labores exant-*
gone, and ended,	*latos*,
being even wearied,	& lassata,
she resteth her self;	quiescit:
but being refreshed with Rest,	Sed, *quiete* recreata,
that she may not use her self to Idleness,	ne adsuescat *Otio*,
she falleth again to her business.	redit ad *Negotia*.
A diligent Scholar	Diligens *Discipulus*,
is like Bees, 8.	similis est *Apibus*, 8.
which carry honey	qui ex variis *Floribus*, 9
from divers flowers 9.	*Mel* congerunt
into their Hive. 10.	in *Alveare* 10. suum,

CXII.

Temperantia.

Temperance.

Temperance 1.	*Temperantia*, 1.
prescribeth a mean	*modum* præscribit
to meat and drink, 2.	*Cibo* & *Potui*, 2.
and restraineth	& continet
the desire	*Cupidinem*
as with a Bridle, 3.	ceu *Freno*, 3.
and so	& sic
moderateth all things	omnia moderatur,
lest any thing too	ne quid nimis fiat.
much be done.	
Revellers	*Heluones* (ganeones)
are made drunk, 4.	*inebriantur*, 4.
they stumble, 5.	*titubant*, 5.
they spue, 6.	*ructant* (vomunt) 6.
and brabble. 7.	& *rixantur*. 7.
From drunkenness	E *Crapulâ*
proceedeth	oritur
lasciviousness;	*Lascivia*;
from this	ex hâc,
a lewd life (sters, 8,	*Vita libidinosa*
amongst Whorema-	inter *Fornicatores* 8.
and Whores, 9.	& *Scorta*, 9,
in kissing,	*Osculando* (basiando)
touching,	*palpando*,
embracing,	*amplexando*,
and dancing. 10.	& *tripudiando*. 10.

CXIII.

Fortitudo.

Fortitude.

For,

Fortitude 1.	*Fortitudo* 1.
is undaunted	impavida est
in adversity,	in adversis,
and bold as a Lion ; 2.	ut *Leo*, 2. & confidens ;
but not haughty	at non tumida
in prosperity,	in Secundis :
leaning	innixa
on her own Pillar 3.	suo *Columini* 3.
Constancy ;	*Constantiæ* ;
and being the same	& eadem
in all things,	in omnibus,
ready to undergo	parata
both estates.	ad utramque *fortunam*
with	æquo animo
an even mind.	ferendam.
She receiveth	*Clypeo* 4.
the strokes	*Tolerantiæ*
of misfortune	excipit
with the Shield 4.	ictûs
of Sufferance :	*Infortunii* :
and keepeth off	& *Gladio* 5.
the Passions,	*Virtutis*,
the enemies	propellit
of quietness,	hostes
with the Sword 5.	*Euthymiæ*,
of Valour.	*Affectûs*.

XC.

Patientia.

Patience.

Patience 1. endureth	*Patientia* 1. tolerat
Calamities 2.	*Calamitates* 2.
& Wrongs, 3. meekly	& *Injurias*, 3. humilitèr
like a Lamb, 4.	ut *Agnus*, 4.
as Gods Fatherly	tanquam paternam
chastisement. 5.	*Dei ferulam.* 5.
In the mean while	Interim innititur
she leaneth upon the	
Anchor of Hope, 6.	*Spei anchoræ*, 6.
(as a Ship 7.	(ut *Navis* 7.
tossed by waves in the Sea)	mari fluctuans)
she prayeth to God 8.	*Deo supplicat* 8.
weeping,	illacrumando,
& expecteth the Sun; 10.	& expectat
after cloudy-weather 9.	post *Nubila* 9.
suffering evils,	*Phœbum*; 10.
and hoping better	ferens mala,
things.	sperans meliora.
On the contrary	Contra
the impatient person 11	*Impatiens* 11.
waileth, lamenteth,	plorat, lamentatur,
rageth against himself,	*in seipsum debacchatur*,
grumbleth like (12.	obmurmurat (12.
a Dog, 13.	ut *Canis*, 13.
and yet doth no good;	& tamen nil proficit;
at the last he despaireth and becometh	tandem desperat,
his own murtherer; 14	& fit *Autochir* : 14.
being full of rage he	Injurias
desireth to revenge	vindicare cupit.
wrongs.	furibundus. Huma-

CXV.

Humanity. *Humanitas.*

Men are made for one anothers good; therefore let them be kind.

Be thou ſweet and lovely in thy countenance: 1. gentle & civil in thy behaviour, & manners, 2 affable & true-ſpoken with thy mouth:

Homines facti ſunt ad mutua *commoda*; ergo ſint *humani*.

Sis ſuavis, & amabilis, *Vultu*: 1. comis & urbanus, *Geſtu* ac *Moribus*: 2. affabilis & verax, *Ore*: 3.

affecti-

affectionate & candid in thy heart. 4.	candens & *candidus Corde.* 4.
So love, and so ſhalt thou be loved;	Sic ama, ſic amaberis;
and there will be a mutual friendſhip, 5.	& fiet mutua *Amicitia,* 5.
as that of Turtle-doves, 6.	ceu *Turturum,* 6.
hearty, gentle,	concors, manſueta;
and wiſhing well on both parts.	& utrinque benevola.
Froward men,	Moroſi homines,
are hateful, teaſty,	ſunt odioſi, torvi,
unpleaſant, contentious,	illepidi, contentioſi,
angry, 7.	*iracundi,* 7.
cruel, 8.	*crudeles* 8.
and implacable,	ac implacabiles,
(rather Wolves and Lyons, than Men)	(magis lupi & leones, quàm homines,)
and ſuch as fall out among themſelves,	& inter ſe diſcordes,
hereupon they fight in a Duel 9.	hinc confligunt *Duello.* 9.
Envy, 10.	*Invidia,* 10.
wiſhing ill to others,	aliis malè cupiendo,
pineth away her ſelf.	ſeipſam conficit.

CXVI.

Justice. Justitia.

Justice 1.
is painted, sitting on
a square Stone; 2.
for she ought to be
immoveable;
with hoodwinked eyes,
that she may not (3.
respect persons;
stopping the left ear, 4.
to be reserved for the
other party;
Holding in her right
hand a sword, 5.
and a Bridle, 6.

Justitia 1.
pingitur, sedens
in *lapide quadrato*: 2.
nam debet esse
immobilis;
obvelatis oculis, 3.
ad non respiciendum
personas; *claudens*
aurem sinistram, 4.
reservandam
alteri parti;
Dexterâ tenens
Gladium, 5.
& *Frænum*, 6.

to

to punish and restrain	ad puniendum
evil men;	& coërcendum Malos;
Besides	Præterea *Statéram*, 7.
a pair of ballances, 7.	cujus *dextræ Lanci* 8.
in the right scale 8.	Merita,
whereof deserts,	*Sinistræ*, 9.
and in the left (9.	*Præmia* imposita,
rewards being put	sibi invicem
are made	exæquantur,
even one with another,	atque ita Boni
and so good Men	ad virtutem,
are incited to virtue as	ceu *Calcaribus*, 10.
it were with Spurs, 10.	incitantur.
In Bargains, 11.	In *Contractibus*, 11.
let men deal candidly;	candidè agatur:
let them stand to their	*Pactis & Promissis*
Covenants & Promises,	stetur:
let that which is given	*Depositum*, *Mutuum*,
one to keep,	
and that which is lent,	reddantur:
be restored; (12.	nemo *expiletur*, 12.
let no man be pillaged,	
or hurt; 13. let every	aut *lædatur*; 13.
one have his own:	suum cuiq; tribuatur:
these are the precepts	hæc sunt præcepta
of Justice.	Justitiæ.
Such things as these	Talia prohibentur,
are forbidden in Gods	*quinto & septimo*
5 & 7 Commandement	*Dei præcepto*,
and deservedly	& meritò
punish'd on the Gollows	*Cruce* ac *Rotâ* 14.
and the Wheel. 14.	puniuntur. *Li-*

CXVII.

Liberalitas.

Liberality.

Liberality 1.	*Liberalitas* 1.
keepeth a mean	modum servat
about Riches,	circa *Divitias*,
which she honestly	
seeketh, that she may	quas honestè quærit,
have somewhat	
to bestow on them	ut habeat quod largia-
that want; 2.	*Egenis*; 2. (tur
She cloatheth, 3.	Hos, *vestit*, 3.
nourisheth, 4.	*nutrit*, 4.
and enricheth 5.	*ditat*, 5.
these with a	
chearful countenance 6	*Vultu hilari*, 6.
and a winged Hand. 7.	& *Manu alatâ*. 7.
She submitteth her	*Opes* 8.
wealth 8. to her self,	sibi subjicit;
not her self to it,	non se illis, ut *Avarus* 9
as the covetuous man, 9	qui habet, ut habeat,
doth, who hath, that he	& bonorum suorum
may have, & is not the	non *Possessor est*
owner, but the keeper of	sed *Custos*,
his goods, & being unsa-	&, insatiabilis,
tiable always scrapeth	semper *corradit*. 10.
together 10. with his	Unguibus suis.
Moreover he (nails,	Sed & parcit
and keepeth, (spareth	& adservat,
Hoarding up 11. (have:	*occludendo*, 11.
that he may alwaies	ut semper habeat:
But the Prodigal 12.	At *Prodigus* 12.
badly spendeth things	male disperdit
well gotten, and at the	benè parta,
last wanteth.	ac tandem eget. The

CXVIII.

The Society betwixt Man and Wife.

Societas Conjugalis.

Marriage
was appointed by God
in Paradise,
for mutual help,
and the Propagation
of man-kind.
A young-man (a single-man)
being to be married,
should be furnished
either with wealth,
or a Trade and Science,
which may serve
for getting a living;
that he may be able to
maintain a Family.

Matrimonium
à Deo est institutum
in Paradiso,
ad *mutuum Adjutorium*,
& *Propagationem*
generis humani.
Vir-Juvenis (*Cœlebs*)
conjugium initurus,
instructus sit
aut *Opibus*,
aut *Arte* & *Scientiâ*,
quæ sit,
de pane lucrendo;
ut possit sustentare
Familiam.

Then

Then he chooseth himself
a Maid that is marriageable
(or a Widdow) whom he
loveth; where nevertheless
a greater regard is to be
had of Vertue and Honesty
than of Beauty
or portion.
Afterwards,
he doth not betroth her to
himself closely,
but intreateth for her
as a woer,
first to the Father, 1.
and then the Mother, 2.
or the Guardians
and kinsfolks, by such as
help to make the match. 3.
When she is espous'd to him
he becometh the bride-
& she the Bride, 5. (groom, 4
& the contract is made,
& an Instrument of the Dow-
ry 6. is written.
At the last
the wedding is made,
where they are joyned
together by the Priest, 7.
giving their Hands 8.
one to another,
and wedding Rings; 9.
then they feast with the
witnesses that are invit'd.
After this they are called
Husband and Wife;
when she is dead he be-
cometh a Widdower.

Deinde eligit sibi
Virginem nubilem,
(aut *Viduam*)
quam adamat: (habenda
ubi tamen major ratio
Virtutis & *Honestatis*,
quàm *Formæ*
aut *Dotis*.
Posthæc,
non clam despondet
sibi eam,
sed ambit,
ut *Procus*,
apud *Patrem* 1.
& *Matrem*, 2.
vel apud *Tutores*
& *Cognatos*,
per *Pronubos*. 3.
Eâ sibi desponsa,
fit *Sponsus*, 4.
& ipsa, *Sponsa*; 5.
fiuntq; *Sponsalia*,
& scribitur
Instrumentum dotale. 6.
Tandem
fiunt *Nuptiæ*,
ubi copulantur
à *Sacerdote*, 7.
datis ultrò citróq;
Manibus 8.
& *Annulis nuptialibus*; 9.
tum epulantur
cum invitatis Testibus.
Abhinc dicuntur
Maritus & *Uxor*;
hâc mortuâ
ille fit *Viduus*.

CXIX.

The tree of Consanguinity. *Arbor Consanguinitatis*

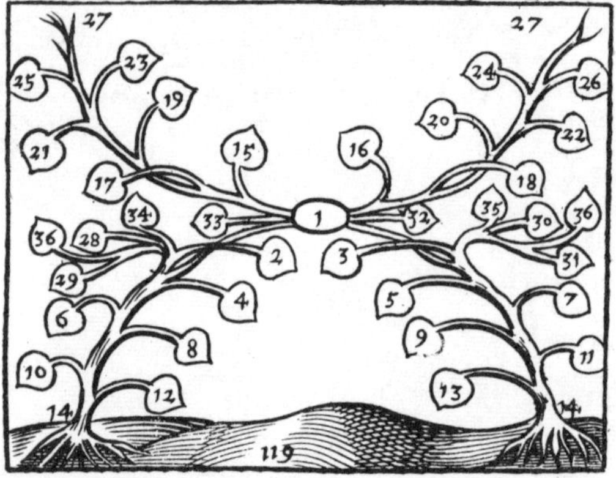

In Consanguinity
there touch a man 1.
in Lineal Ascent,
the Father (the Father
in Law) 2.
and the Mother (the
Mother in Law,) 3.
the Grand-father, 4.
& the Grand-mother, 5.
the great-grandfather
& the great-grand- (6.
mother, 7. the great-
great-grand-father, 8.
the great-great-grand-
mother, 9. the great-
great-grand-fathers
Father, 10.

Hominem 1. (gunt,
Consanguinitate attin-
in *Lineâ Ascendenti,*
Pater
(*Vitricus*) 2.
& *Mater*
(*Noverca*) 3.
Avus; 4.
& *Avia*, 5.
Proavus 6.
& *Proavia*, 7.
Abavus 8.
& *Abavia*, 9.
Atavus 10.

the

the great-great-grand-mothers Mother, 11.	& *Atavia*, 11.
the great-great-grand-fathers-grand-Father, 12.	*Tritavus* 12.
the great-great-grand-mothers-grandmothers 13.	& *Tritavia* ; 13.
These beyond these are called ancestors. 14... 14.	Ulteriores dicuntur *Majores*. 14... 14
In a Lineal descent,(15 the son (the son in Law) **and** the daughter (the daughter in Law, 16.)	In *Lineâ descendenti*, *Filius (Privignus)* 15. & *Filia (Privigna)* 16.
the Nephew 17.	*Nepos* 17.
and the Neece, 18.	& *Neptis*, 18.
the Nephews Son 19.	*Pronepos* 19.
& theNephewsDaughter 20.	& *Proneptis*, 20.
the Nephews Nephew, 21.	*Abnepos*, 21.
& the Neeces Neece, 22.	& *Abneptis*, 22.
the Nephews Nephews Son 23.	*Atnepos*, 23
the Neeces Neeces daughter, 24.	& *Atneptis*, 24.
the Nephews Nephews Nephew. 25.	*Trinepos* 25.
the Neeces Neeces Neece, 26.	& *Trineptis* ; 26.
Those beyond these are called Posterity. 27...27.	Ulteriores dicuntur *Posteri*. 27... 27.
In a Collateral Line **are** theUncle by thefathers side 28	In *Linea Collaterali* sunt *Patruus* 28.
and theAunt by the fathers side, 29.	& *Amita*, 29.
the Uncle by the Mothers side, 30.	*Avunculus* 30.
and the Aunt by the Mothers side, 31.	& *Matertera*, 31.
the Brother (32.	*Frater* 32.
and the Sister, 33.	& *Soror*, 33.
the Brothers Son, 34.	*Patruelis*, 34.
the SistersSon,35	*Sobrinus*, 35.
& the cosin by the Brother and Sister.36.	& *Amitinus*. 36.36.

CXX.

Societas Parentalis.

The Society betwixt Parents, and Children.

The

Married Persons,	*Conjuges*, suscipiunt
(by the blessing of God)	(ex benedictione Dei)
have issue,	*Sobolem* (Prolem)
and become Parents.	& fiunt *Parentes*.
The Father 1. beget-	*Pater* 1. generat,
teth, and the Mother 2.	& *Mater* 2.
beareth Sons, 3.	parit *Filios* 3.
and Daughters, 4.	& *Filias*, 4.
(sometimes Twins.)	(aliquando *Gemellos*.)
The Infant 5.	*Infans* 5.
is wrapped in	
Swadling-clothes, 6.	involvitur *Fasciis*, 6.
is laid in a Cradle, 7.	reponitur in *Cunas*. 7.
is suckled by the Mo-	à matre
ther with her breasts, 8.	lactatur *Uberibus*, 8.
and fed with Pap. 9.	& nutritur *Pappis*. 9.
Afterwards	Deinde,
it learneth to go by	incedére discit
a Standing stool, 10.	*Serperastro*, 10.
playeth with Rattles, 11	ludit *Crepundiis*, 11.
& beginneth to speak.	& fari incipit.
As it beginneth to	Crescente ætate,
grow older, it is accu-	
stomed to Piety 12.	*Pietati* 12.
and Labour, 13.	& *Labori* 13. adsuefit,
and is chastised 14.	& castigatur 14.
if it be not dutiful.	si non sit morigerus.
Children owe to Pa-	*Liberi* debent
rents Reverence,	Parentibus
and Service.	Cultum & Officium.
The Father main-	Pater,
taineth his Children	sustentat Liberos,
by taking Pains. 15.	*laborando*. 15. *Socie-*

CXXI.

Societas herilis.

The Society betwixt Masters and Servants.

The Maſter (the good-man of the Houſe) 1.	*Herus (Pater-familias)* 1.
hath Men-Servants; 2.	habet *Famulos (Servos)* 2.
the Miſtreſs (the good wife of the Houſe) 3.	*Hera (Mater famili-as)* 3.
Maidens. 4.	*Ancillas* 4.
They appoint theſe their Work, 6.	Illi mandant his *Opera*, 6.
and divide them their Tasks; 5.	& diſtribuunt *Laborum penſa*; 5.
which are faithfully to be done by them	quæ ab his fideliter ſunt exſequenda,
without Murmuring, and loſs;	ſine Murmure & Diſpendio;
for which their Wages, and Meat and Drink is allowed them.	pro quo præbetur ipſis, *Merces* & *Alimonia*.
A Servant was heretofore a Slave,	*Servus* olim erat *Mancipium*,
over whom the Maſter had power of life and death.	in quem Vitæ & necis Domino poteſtas fuit:
At this day the poorer ſort ſerve in a free manner,	Hodiè Serviunt libere pauperiores,
being hired for wages.	mercede conducti.

CXXII.

A City. *Urbs.*

Of many Houses	Ex multis Domibus
is made a Village, 1.	fit *Pagus*, 1.
or a Town,	vel *Oppidum*,
or a City. 2.	vel *Urbs*. 2.
That and this	Istud & hæc (tur
are fenced and begirt	muniuntur & cingun-
with a Wall 3.	*Mœnibus* (*muro*) 3.
a Trench, 4.	*Vallo*, 4.
Bulwarks 5.	*Aggeribus* 5.
and Palisadoes. 6.	& *Vallis*. 6.
Within the walls	Intra muros,
is the voyd Place; 7.	est *Pomœrium*; 7.

with-

without,	extra,
the Ditch. 8.	*Fossa.* 8.
In the walls	In mœnibus,
are Fortresses 9.	sunt *Propugnacula* 9.
and Towers; 10.	& *Turres*; 10.
Watch-towers 11.	*Specula* 11.
are upon	exstant
the higher places.	in editioribus locis.
The entrance into	In Urbem
a City is made	ingressus fit,
out of the Suburbs, 12	ex *Suburbio.* 12.
through the Gate, 13.	per *Portam*, 13.
over the Bridge. 14.	super *Pontem.* 14.
The Gate hath	*Porta* habet
a Percullis, 15.	*Cataractas*, 15.
a Draw Bridge, 16.	*Pontem versatilem*, 16.
two-leaved Doors, 17.	*Valvas*, 17.
Locks,	*Claustra*,
and Bolts,	& *Repagula*,
as also	ut &
Barres. 18.	*Vectes.* 18.
In the Suburbs	In Suburbiis
are Gardens, 19.	sunt *Horti*, 19.
and Garden-houses, 20	& *Suburbana*, 20.
and also	ut &
Burying-places. 21.	*Cœmeteria.* 21.

CXXIII.

The inward parts of a City.

Interiora Urbis.

Within a City
are Streets, 1.
paved with stones;
Market-places, 2.
(in some places
with Galleries) 3.
and narrow Lanes, 4.
The publick buildings
are in the middle of the
the Church, 5. (City,
the School, 6.
the Guild-hall, 7.
the Exchange. 8.

Intra Urbem
sunt *Plateæ* (Vici) 1.
lapidibus stratæ:
Fora, 2.
(alicubi
cum *Porticibus*) 3.
& *Angiportis*. 4.
Publica ædificia sunt
in medio Urbis,
Templum, 5.
Schola, 6.
Curia, 7.
Domus Mercaturæ: 8.

About

About the walls,	Circa Mænia,
and the Gates,	& Portas,
are the Magazine, 9.	*Armamentarium*, 9.
the Granary, 10.	*Granarium*, 10.
Innes,	*Diversoria*,
Ale-houses,	*Popinæ*,
Cooks-shops, 11	& *Cauponæ*, 11.
the Play-house, 12.	*Theatrum*, 12.
and the Spittle; 13.	*Nosodochium*; 13.
In the by-places	In recessibus,
are houses of office, 14.	*Foricæ* (Cloacæ) 14.
and the Prison. 15.	& *Custodia*(Carcer)15.
In the chief Steeple	In Turre primariâ
is the Clock, 16.	est *Horologium*, 16.
and the Watchmens	& habitatio
dwelling. 17.	*Vigilum*. 17.
In the Streets	In Plateis
are Wells. 18.	sunt *Putei*. 18.
The River 19.	*Fluvius*, 19.
or Beck	vel *Rivus*,
runing about the City,	Urbem interfluens,
serveth	inservit
to wash away the filth.	*sordibus* eluendis.
The Tower 10.	*Arx* 20.
standeth in the highest	exstat
part of the City.	in summo Urbis.

CXXIV.

Judicium.

Judgment

The

The best Law is
a quiet agreement,
made either
by themselves, (is,
betwixt whom the sute
or by an Umpire.
If this do not proceed
they come into Court. 1.
(heretofore they judg'd
in the Market-pl. (hall)
at this day in the Moot-
in which the Judge 2. (3
sitteth with his Assessors
the Clerk 4. (writing.
taketh their votes in
The plaintiff 5.
accuseth
the Defendant, 6. (7.
& produceth witnesses
against him. (cuseth
The Defendant ex-
himself by a counselor,
whom the Plaintiffs (8
Counselor 9. contra-
Then the Judg (dicts.
pronounceth Sentence,
acquitting the innocent,
and condemning him
that is guilty (fine,
to a punishment, or a
or torment.

Optimum *Jus* est
placida *conventio*,
facta,
vel ab ipsis,
inter quos Lis est,
vel ab *Arbitro*
Hæc si non procedit,
venitur in *Forum*, 1.
(olim judicabant
in Foro,
hodiè in *Prætorio*)
cui præsidet *Judex* [Præ-
cu *Assessoribus*, 3. (tor] 2
Dicographus, 4.
Vota calamo excipit.
Actor 5.
accusat
Reum, 6.
& producit *Testes* 7.
contra illum.
Reus excusat se
per *Advocatum*; 8.
cui contradicit
Actoris *Procurator*. 9.
Tum *Judex*
Sententiam pronunciat,
absolvens *insontem*,
& damnans *sontem*
ad *Pœnam*, vel *Mul-
ctam*,
vel ad *Supplicium*.

Mar-

CXXV.

The tormenting of Malefactors. — *Supplicia Maleficorum.*

Malefactors 1.
are brought from the
Prison, 3. (where they
are wont to be tortu-
by Sergeants, 2. (red)
or drag'd with a horse 15
to place of Execution.
Theeves 4.
are hanged
by the Hangman, 6.
on a Gallows; 5.
Whore-masters
are beheaded; 7.

Malefici 1.
per *Lictores*, 2.
è *Carcere* 3.
(ubi torqueri solent)
producuntur,
vel *equo raptantur*, 15.
ad locum *Supplicii*.
Fures, 4.
in *Patibulo* 5.
suspenduntur
à *Carnifice*; 6.
Mœchi
decollantur

Mur-

Murtherers
and Robbers
are either laid upon
a Wheel, 8. (ken,
having their Legs bro-
or fastned upon a stake.
Witches (9.
are burnt in
a great Fire. 10.
Some before they be
executed have their
tongues cut out, 11.
or have their Hand 13.
cut off upon a Block, 12
or are burnt
with Pincers. 14.
They that have their
life given them,
are set on the Pillory,
are strapadoed, 17. (16.
are set upon a wooden-
horse, 18.
have their ears cut off,
are whipped, 20. (19.
are branded,
are banished,
are condemned,
to the galleys, (sonmet.
or to perpetual impri-
Traytors are pulled in
pieces with 4 horses.

Homicidæ (Sicarii)
ac *Latrones* (Piratæ)
vel *crurifragio plexi*
Rotæ imponuntur, 8.
vel *Palo* infiguntur; 9.
Striges (Lamiæ)
super *Rogum* 10.
cremantur.
Quidam (ficiantur
antequam supplicio af-
elinguantur, 11.
aut super *Cippum* 12.
Manu plectuntur, 13.
aut *Forcipibus* 14.
uruntur.
Vitâ donati,
Numellis constringun-
(tur, 16.
luxantur, 17.
Equuleo imponun-
tur, 18.
Auribus truncantur, 19.
Virgis cæduntur, 20.
Stigmate notantur,
relegantur,
damnantur
ad *triremes*, (petuum.
vel ad Carcerem per-
Perduelles (tur.
quadrigis discerpun-

Mer

CXXVI.

Mercatura.

Merchandizing.

Wares

Wares (places,	*Merces*
brought from other	aliunde allatæ,
are either exchanged	in *domo commerciorum* 1.
in an Exchange, 1.	vel commutantur,
or exposed to sale	vel venum exponuntur
in Warehouses, 2.	in *Tabernis mercimonio-*
and they are sold	& venduntur (*rum*, 2.
for Money, 3.	pro *pecuniâ*(moneta) 3.
being either measured	vel mensuratæ
with an Eln, 4.	*Ulnâ* 4.
or weighed in	vel ponderatæ
a pair of ballances. 5.	*Librâ.* 5.
Shop keepers, 6.	*Tabernarii*, 6.
Pedlars, 7.	*Circumforanei*, 7.
and Brokers, 8	& *Scrutarii*, 8.
would also	etiam volunt
be called Merchants 9.	dici *Mercatores.* 9.
The Seller	*Venditor*
braggeth of a thing	ostentat
that is to be sold,	rem promercalem,
& setteth the rate of it,	& indicat pretium,
and how much it may	quanti liceat.
be sold for.	
The Buyer 10.	*Emptor* 10.
cheapneth,	licitatur,
and offereth the price.	& pretium offert.
If any one	Si quis
bid against him, 11.	*contralicetur*, 11.
the thing is delivered	ei res addicitur,
to him that promiseth	qui plurimum
the most.	pollicetur.

CXXVII.

Mensuræ & Pondera.

Measures and Weights.

We measure things	Res continuas,
that hang together with	metimur *Ulnâ*, 1.
liquid (an Eln, 1.	liquidas,
things with a Gallon, 2.	*Congio*, 2.
dry things by (3.	aridas,
two-bushel measure.	*Medimno*. 3.
We try the heaviness	Gravitatem rerum
of things by Weights 4.	experimur *Ponderibus* 4.
and Ballances. 5.	& *Librâ* (bilance) 5.
In this is first	In hâc primo est
the Beam ; 6.	*Jugum* (Scapus) 6.
In the midst whereof is	in cujus medio
a little Axle-tree, 7.	*Axiculus*, 7.
above,	superius
the cheeks & the hole, 8.	*Trutina* & *agina* 8.
in which the Needle 9.	in quâ *Examen* 9.
moveth it self to & fro :	sese agitat :
on both sides	utrinque
are the Scales, 10.	sunt *Lances*, 10.
hanging by	pendentes
little Cords. 11.	*Funiculis*. 11.
The Brasiers ballance 12	*Statera* 12.
weigheth things,	ponderat res,
by hanging them	suspendendo illas
on a Hook, 13.	*Unco*, 13.
and the Weight 14.	& *Pondus* 14.
opposite to them, which	ex opposito,
in (a) weigheth just	quod in (*a*)
as much as the thing,	æquiponderat rei,
in (b) twice so much,	in (*b*) bis tantum,
in (c) thrice so much, &c.	in (*c*) ter, *&c.*

CXXVIII.

Ars Medica.

Physick.

Th

The Patient 1. (2.	*Ægrotans*, 1.
sendeth for a physitian	accersit *Medicum* 2.
who feeleth	qui tangit
his Pulse, 3.	ipsius *Arteriam*, 3.
and looketh upon	& inspicit
his Water, 4	*Urinam*, 4
and then prescribeth	tum præscribit
a Receipt	*Medicamentum*
in a Bill 5.	in *Schedulâ* 5.
That is made ready	Istud paratur
by the Apothecary 6.	à *Pharmacopæo* 6.
in an Apothecaries	in *Pharmacopolio*, 7.
shop, 7.	ubi *Pharmaca*
where Drugs	in *Capsulis*, 8.
are kept in Drawers, 8.	*Pyxidibus*, 9.
Boxes, 9.	& *Lagenis* 10.
and Galley pots 10.	adservantur.
And it is either	Estq;
a Potion, 11.	vel *Potio*, 11.
or Powder, 12.	vel *Pulvis*, 12.
or Pills, 13.	vel *Pillulæ*, 13.
or Trochisks, 14.	vel *Pastilli*, 14.
or an Electuary. 15.	vel *Electuarium*. 15.
Diet	*Diæta*
and Prayer, 16	& *Oratio*, 16.
is the best Physick.	est optima *Medicina*.
The Chirurgion 18.	*Chirurgus* 18.
cureth Wounds 17.	curat *Vulnera* 17.
and Ulcers,	& *Ulcera*,
with Plaisters. 19.	*Spleniis* (*emplastris*.) 19.

CXXIX.

Sepultura.

A Burial.

Dead

Dead Folks (burned,	*Defuncti*
heretofore were	olim cremabantur,
and their ashes	& Cineres
put into	in *Urnâ* 1.
an Urn. 1.	recondebantur.
We enclose	Nos includimus
our dead Folks,	nostros *demortuos*,
in a Coffin 2.	*Loculo* (*Capulo*) 2.
lay them upon a Bier, 3.	imponimus *Feretro*, 3.
and see they be carried	& efferri curamus
out in a Funeral-pomp	*Pompâ funebri*
towards the Church-	versus *Cœmeterium*, 4.
where they are (yard, 4.	ubi
laid into the Grave, 6.	à *Vespillonibus* 5.
by the Bearers 5.	inferuntur *Sepulchro*, 6.
and are interred;	& humantur;
this is covered	hoc *Cippo* 7.
with a Grave-stone 7.	tegitur,
and is adorned	& *Monumentis* 8.
with Tombs, 8.	ac *Epitaphiis* 9.
and Epitaphs 9.	ornatur.
As the Corps	Funere
go along,	prodeunte,
Psalms are sung,	cantantur *Hymni*,
and the Bells	& *Campanæ* 10.
are rung. 10.	pulsantur.

CXXX.

Ludus Scenicus.

A Stage-Play.

In a Play-house, 1.	In *Theatro*, 1.
which is trimmed	(quod vestitur
with Hangings, 2.	*Tapetibus*, 2.
and covered with	
Curtains, 3.	& *Sipariis* 3.
Comedies,	tegitur)
& Tragedies	aguntur *Comœdiæ*
are acted,	vel *Tragœdiæ*,
wherein memorable	quibus representantur
things are represen-	res memorabiles;
ted; as here,	ut hic,
the History	Historia
of the Prodigal Son, 4.	de *Filio prodigo*, 4.
and his Father, 5.	& *Patre* 5. ipsius,
by whom	à quo
he is entertained,	recipitur,
being returned home.	domum redux.
The Players	*Actores* (*Histriones*)
act	agunt
being in disguise;	personati:
the Fool, 6.	*Morio*, 6.
maketh Jests.	dat Jocos.
The chief of the	Spectatorum
Spectators sit in	primarii,
the Gallery, 7.	sedent in
the common sort	*Orchestrâ*: 7.
stand in the ground, 8.	Plebs stat
and clap their hands	in *Caveâ*, 8.
if any thing	& plaudit,
please them.	si quid arridet.

Præstigiæ.

CXXXI.

Præstigiæ:

Sleights.

The Tumbler 1.	*Præstigiator* 1.
maketh	facit
several Shows,	varia *Spectacula*,
by the nimbleness	volubilitate
of his body,	corporis,
walking to and fro	deambulando
on his hands,	*manibus*,
leaping through	saliendo
a Hoop, 2. &c.	per *Circulum*, 2. &c.
Sometimes also	Interdum etiam
he danceth 4.	*tripudiat* 4.
having on a vizzard.	larvatus.
The Jugler 3	*Agyrta* 3.
sheweth sleights,	*Præstigias* facit,
out of a Purse.	è *marsupio*,
The Rope-dancer 5.	*Funambulus*, 5.
goeth and danceth	graditur & saltat
upon a Rope,	super *funem*,
holdeth a Poise 6.	tenens manu
in his Hand;	*Halterem*; 6.
or hangeth himself	aut suspendit se
by the Hand	*manu*
or Foot, 7. &c.	vel *Pede*, 7. &c.

CXXXII.

Palæstra.

The Fencing School.

Fencers	*Pugiles*
meet in a Duel	congrediuntur Duello
in a Fencing-place,	in *Palæstrâ*, decertantes
fighting with swords 1.	vel *Gladiis*, 1.
or Pikes 2.	vel *Hastilibus* 2.
and Halberds, 3.	& *Bipennibus*, 3.
or Short-swords, 4.	vel *Semispathis*, 4.
or Rapiers 5.	vel *Ensibus* 5.
having Bals at the point	*mucronem obligatus*,
(lest they wound one another mortally,)	ne lethaliter lædant,
or with	
two edged-swords	vel *Frameis*
and a Daggar 6.	& *Pugione* 6.
together.	simul.
Wrastlers 7.	*Luctatores* 7.
(among the Romans	(apud Romanos
in times past	olim nudi
were naked, & anointed with Oyl)	& inuncti oleo)
take hold of one another,	prehendunt se invicem
and strive	& annituntur,
whether	uter alterum
can throw the other,	prosternere possit,
especially by tripping,	præprimis
up his heels. 8.	*supplantando.* 8.
Hood-winked fencers 9	*Andabatæ* 9.
fought with their fists	pugnabant Pugnis,
in a ridiculous strife,	ridiculo certamine,
to wit, with their	nimirùm
eyes covered.	obvelatis oculis.

Ludus

CXXXIII.

Ludus Pilæ.

Tennis-Play.

In

In a Tennis-Court, 1.
they play
with a Ball, 2.
which one throweth,
and another taketh,
& sendeth it back with
a Racket: 3.
and that is the sport
of Noble-men
to stir their body.

A wind-ball 4.
being filled with air
by means of a Ventil,
is tossed to and fro
with the Fist 5.
in the open air.

In *Sphæristerio*, 1.
luditur
Pilâ, 2.
quam alter mittit,
alter excipit,
& remittit
Reticulo: 3.
idque est Lusus
Nobilium (poris.
ad commotionem cor-

Follis (pila magna) 4.
aere distenta
ope *Epistomii*,
sub dio
Pugno 5.
reverberatur.

CXXXIV.

Ludus Aleæ.

Dice-Play.

We play with Dice 1.	*Tesseris* (*talis*) 1.
either they that throw	ludimus,
the most take up all ;	vel *Plistobolindam* ;
or we throw them thorow a casting-Box 2.	vel immittimus illas per *Fritillum* 2.
upon a Board 3.	in *Tabellam* 3.
marked with Figures;	numeris notatam,
and this is	idque est
Dice-players game	Ludus *Sortilegii*
at casting Lots.	*Aleatorum*.
Men play by	*Sorte* & *Arte*
Luck and Skill	luditur
at Tables	*Calculis*
in a pair of Tables, 4.	in *alveo aleatorio*, 4.
and at Cards. 5.	& *Chartis lusoriis*. 5.
We play at Chesse	*Abaculis*
on a Chesse-board, 6.	ludimus in *Abaco*, 6.
where only art	ubi sola ars
beareth the sway.	regnat.
The most	Ingeniosissimus
ingenious Game,	ludus est,
is the game at Chess, 7.	L. *Latrunculorum*, 7.
wherein as it were	quo veluti
two Armies fight	duo exercitûs
together in Battel.	prælio confligunt.

CXXXV.

Curſûs Certamina.

Races,

Boyes exercise themselves in running either upon the Ice, 1. in Scrick shooes, 2. where they are carried also upon Sleds; 3. or in the open field making a Line, 4. which, he that desireth to win, ought to touch, but not to run beyond it.

Heretofore Runners, 5. ran betwixt Railes 6. to the Goal, 7. and he that touched it first, received the prize 8. from him that gave the prize. 9.

At this day Tilting (or the quintain) is used; where a Hoop 11. is struck at with a Truncheon, 10. instead of Horse-races, which are grown out of use.

Pueri exercent se cursu, sive super *Glaciem* 1. *Diabatris*, 2. ubi etiam vehuntur *Trahis*; 3. sive in campo designantes *Lineam*, 4. quam, qui vincere cupit, adtingere, at non ultrà procurrere, debet.

Olim decurrebant *Cursores* 5. inter *Cancellos* 6. ad *Metam*, 7. & qui primùm contingebat eam, accipiebat *Brabéum (præmium)* 8. à *Brabeutâ*. 9.

Hodie habentur *Hastiludia*, (ubi *Lanceâ* 10. petitur *Circulus* 11.) loco *Equiriorum* quæ in desuetudinem (abierunt.

CXXXVI.

Ludi Pueriles.

Boyes-Sport

Boyes
use to play either with
Bowling-stones ; 1.
or throwing
a Bowl 2.
at Nine-pins ; 3.
or striking a Ball
throw a Ring, 5,
with a Bandy ; 4.
or scourging a Top 6.
with a Whip ; 7.
or shooting with
a Trunck, 8.
and a Bow ; 9.
or going upon
Stilts ; 10.
or tossing
and swinging
themselves upon
a Merry-totter. 11.

Pueri
ludere solent,
vel *globis fictilibus* ; 1.
vel jactantes
Globum 2.
ad *Conas* ; 3.
vel *Spærulam*
Clavâ 4. mittentes
per *Annulum* ; 5.
vel *Turbinem* 6.
Flagello 7.
versantes ;
vel *Sclopo*, 8.
& *Arcu* 9.
jaculantes ;
vel *Grallis* 10.
incedentes ;
vel super *Petaurum* 11.
se agitantes
& oscillantes.

CXXXVII.

Regnum & Regio.

The Kingdom and the Region.

Many Cities
and Villages
make
a Region
and a Kingdom.
The King,
or Prince,
resideth
in the chief-City; 1.
the Noblemen,
Lords,
and Earls,
dwell
in the Castles 2. that lye
round about it;
the Countrey-people
dwell in Villages. 3.
He hath his toll places
upon navigable Rivers,
and High-Roads, 5. (4.
where
Portage
and Tollage
is exacted
of them
that Sayl
or Travel.

Multæ *Urbes*
& *Pagi*
faciunt
Regionem
& *Regnum.*
Rex,
aut *Princeps*
sedet
in *Metropoli*; 1.
Nobiles,
Barones,
& *Comites*,
habitant
in circumjacentibus
Arcibus; 2.
Rustici
in *Pagis*. 3.
Juxta
Flumina navigabilia 4.
& *Vias Regias*, 5.
habet
sua *Telonia*,
ubi
à navigantibus
& iter facientibus,
Portorium
& *Vectigal*
exigitur.

CXXXVIII.

Regal Majesty. *Regia Majestas.*

The King, 1.
sitteth on his throne 2.
in Kingly State,
with a stately Habit, 3.
crowned with Diademe
holding a Scepter, 5. (4.
in his Hand,
being attended with a
company of Courtiers.
The chief,
amongst these, are
the Chancellor 6.
with the Counsellors

Rex, 1.
in splendore regio,
sedet in suo *Solio*, 2.
magnifico *Habitu*, 3.
redimitus *Diademate* 4.
tenens manu
Sceptrum, 5.
stipatus
frequentiâ *Aulicorum.*
Inter hos
primarii sunt,
Cancellarius 6.
cum *Consiliariis*

and

and Secretaries,
the Lord Marshal, 7.
the Comptroller, 8.
the Cup-bearer, 9.
the Taster, 10.
the Treasurer, 11. (12.
the high Chamberlain,
& the Mast. of the horse
There are (13.
subordinate to these,
the Noble Courtiers, 14
the Noble Pages, 15.
with the Chamberlains,
and Lacquies, 16.
the Guard, 17.
with their Attendance.
He solemnly giveth
audience to the Ambas-
sadors of forein Prin-
He sendeth (ces. 18.
his Vice-gerents,
Deputies,
Governors, Treasu-
and Ambassadors (rers
to other places,
to whom he sendeth
new Commissions ever
& anon by the Posts. 19.
The Fool 20.
causeth laughter
by his toysom actions.

& *Secretariis*,
Præfectus Prætorii, 7,
Aulæ-Magister, 8.
Pocillator (pincerna) 9.
Dapifer, 10.
Thesaurarius, 11.
Archi-Cubicularius, 12.
& *Stabuli Magister*. 13

His subordinantur
Nobiles Aulici, 14.
Nobile Famulitium, 15
cum *Cubiculariis*,
& *Cursoribus*, 16.
Stipatores, 17.
cum *Satellitio*.
Legatis Exterorum 18
præbet aures
solenniter.
Aliorsum ablegat
Vicarios suos
Administratores,
Præfectos, *Quæstores*,
& *Legatos*,
quibus subinde mittit
Mandata nova
per *Veredarios*. 19.

Morio, 20.
ludicris actionibus
risum movet.

The

CXXXIX.

The Souldier. *Miles.*

If we be to make war,	Si bellandum est,
Souldiers are listed. 1.	scribuntur *Milites*. 1.
Their Arms are,	Horum *Arma* sunt,
a Head-piece, 2.	*Galea* (Cassis) 2.
(which is adorned with	(quæ ornatur
a Crest)	*Cristâ*)
and the Armour,	*Armatura*,
whose parts are,	cujus partes,
a Collar, 3.	*Torquis ferreus*, 3.
a Brest plate, 4.	*Thorax*, 4.
Arm-pieces, 5.	*Brachialia*,
Leg pieces, 6.	*Ocreæ ferreæ*, 6.
Greaves, 7.	*Manicæ*, 7.
with a Coat of Mail; 8.	cum *Loricâ* 8.
and a Buckler, 9	& *Scuto* (Clypeo) 9.
these are the defensive Arms.	hæc sunt Arma defensiva.
The offensive are,	Offensiva sunt,

A Sword, 10.	*Gladius*, 10.
a two edged Sword, 11.	*Framea*, 11.
a Falchion, 12.	& *Acinaces*, 12.
which are put up	
into a Scabberd, 13.	qui *Vaginâ*, 13.
and are girded	reconduntur,
with a Girdle, 14.	& *Cingulo*, 14. (guntur;
or Belt; 15.	vel *Baltheo*, 15. accin-
(a Scarf, 16.	(*Fascia militaris* 16.
serveth for ornament)	inservit ornatui)
a two-hand-sword, 17.	*Romphaea* 17.
and a Dagger. 18.	& *Pugio*. 18.
In these is	In his est
the Haft, 19.	*Manubrium*, 19.
with the Pummel, 20.	cum *Pomo*, 20.
and the Blade, 21.	& *Verutum*, 21.
having a Point, 22.	*Cuspidatum* 22.
in the middle are (24.	in medio
the Back, 23. & the Edge,	*Dorsum*, 23. & *Acies*. 24.
The other weapons are	Reliqua arma sunt
a Pike, 25. a Halbert,	*Hasta*. 25. *Bipennis*, 26.
in which is (26	in quibus
the Haft, 27. & the Head,	*Hastile* 27. & *Mucro*,
a Club, 29. (28.	*Clava*. 29. (28.
and a Whirlebat. 30.	& *Cæstus* 30.
They fight at a distance	Eminùs pugnatur
with Muskets, 31.	*Bombardis* (Sclopetis) 31
& Pistols, 32. (bullets 33	& *Sclopis*, 32. (33
which are charg'd with	quæ onerantur *Globis*
out of a bullet-bag, 34.	è *Thecâ bombardicâ* 34.
and with Gun-powder	& *pulvere nitrato*
out of a Bandalier, 35.	è *Pyxide pulverariâ* 35.

Castra

CXL.

Castra.

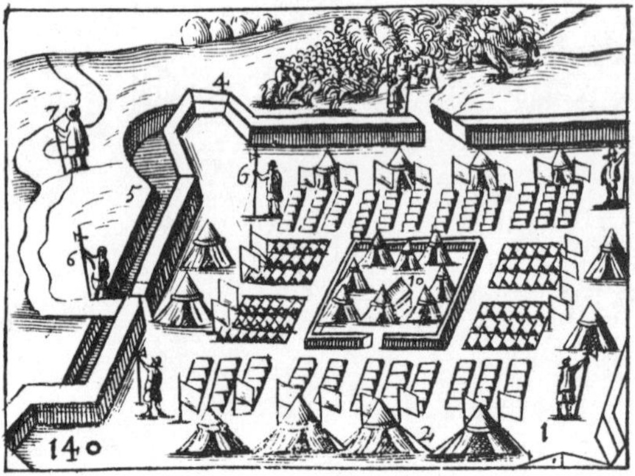

The Camps.

When a Design is
undertaken,
the Camp, 1.
is pitched,
and the Tents
of Canvas 2.
or Straw, 3.
are fastned with stakes,
& they entrench them
about, for securities
with Bulwarks, 4. (sake,
and Ditches ; 5.
Sentinels, 6.
are also set,
and Scouts 7.
are sent out.

Expeditione susce-
ptâ,
Castra 1.
locantur.
& *Tentoria*
paxillis figuntur,
è *Linteis* 2.
vel *Stramentis* ; 3.
eaque circumdant,
securitatis gratiâ,
Aggeribus 4.
& *Fossis* ; 5.
constituuntur etiam
Excubia 6.
& emittuntur
Exploratores. 7.

Sallyings-out 8.
are made
for forrage
and plunder-sake,
where they often cope
with the Enemy 9.
in skirmishing.

Pabulationis
& Prædæ causâ,
fiunt
Excursiones, 8.
ubi sæpius
cum *Hostibus* 9.
velitando confligitur.

The Lord Generals
Pavilion 10.
is in the midst
of the Camp.

Tentorium
summi Imperatoris, 10.
est in medio
Castrorum.

The

CXLI.

The Army, and the Fight. *Acies & Prælium.*

When the Battel is to be fought, (order, the Army is set in and divided into the Front, 1. the Rere, 2. and the Wings. 3.
The Foot 4. are intermixed with the Horse. 5.
That is divided into Companies, this into Troops.
These carry Banners, 6 these Flags 7. in the midst of them.
Their Officers are, Corporals,

Quando *pugna* committenda est, instruitur *Acies*, & dividitur in *Frontem*, 1. *Tergum*, 2. & *Alas* (*Cornua*. 3.
Peditatus 4. intermiscetur *Equitatui*. 5.
Ille distinguitur, in *Centurias*, hic, in *Turmas*.
illæ in medio ferunt *Vexilla*; 6. hæ, *Labara*. 7.
Eorum Præfecti sunt, *Decuriones*, En-

Ensignes,	*Signiferi,*
Lieutenants,	*Vicarii,*
Captains, 8. (horse,9	*Centuriones,* 8.
Commanders of the	*Magistri Equitum,* 9.
Lieutenant Coronels,	*Tribuni,*
Coronels.	*Chiliarchæ,*
& he that is the chief of	& omnium summus
the General. (all	*Imperator.*
The Drummers 10.	*Tympanistæ* 10.
and the Drumslades 11.	& *Tympanotribæ* 11.
as also the Trumpeters	ut & *Tubicines* 12.
call to Arms, (12.	ad arma vocant
and inflame the Soul-	& militem inflammant.
At the first onset (dier.	Primo conflictu,
the Muskets, 13.	exploduntur
and Ordinance 14.	*Bombardæ* 13.
are shot off.	& *Tormenta.* 14.
Afterwards	posteà
they fight 15.	cominùs pugnatur
hand to hand with	*Hastis* & *Gladiis.*
Pikes and Swords.	
They that are	*Victi,*
overcome are slain,16.	*trucidantur,* 16.
or taken prisoners,	vel capiuntur,
or run away. 17.	vel *aufugiunt.* 17.
They that are for the	*Succenturiati,* 18.
reserve, 18,	superveniunt
come upon them	ex *insidiis.*
out of their places	
where they lay in wait	
The Carriages are 19.	*Impedimenta* 19.
plundered.	spoliantur

Pugna

CXLII.

Pugna Navalis.

The Sea fight.

A Sea-fight	*Navale prælium*
is terrible	terribile est,
when	quum
huge Ships	ingentes *Naves*,
like Castles,	veluti *Arces*,
run one upon another	concurrunt
with their Beaks, 1.	*Rostris*, 1.
or shatter one another	
with their Ordnance, 2.	aut *Tormentis*, 2.
and so being	se invicem quassant
bored thorow,	atque ita perforatæ,
they drink in their	perniciem suam
own destruction,	imbibunt
and are Sunk : 3.	& *submerguntur* : 3.
Or when	Aut, quum
they are set on fire,	igne corripiuntur,
and either	& vel
by the firing	ex incendio
of Gun-Powder, 4.	*pulveris tormentarii*, 4.
men are blown up,	homines
into the air,	in aërem ejiciuntur,
and are burnt	vel in mediis aquis
in the midst	exuruntur,
of the waters,	vel etiam
or else	in mare desilientes
leaping into the Sea	suffocantur.
are drowned.	
A Ship that flieth (away 5.	*Navis fugitiva* 5.
is overtaken by those	ab *insequentibus* 6.
that pursue her, 6.	intercipitur
and is taken.	& capitur.

U The

CXLIII.

The Besieging of a City.

Obsidium Urbis.

A City that is like
to endure a Siege,
is first Summoned
by a Trumpeter, 1.
and perswaded
to Yeild.
Which if it
refuse to do,
it is assaulted
by the Besiegers,
and taken by Storm:
Either by climbing
over the Walls
with Scaling-ladders 2.

Urbs
obsidionem passura,
primùm provocatur
per *Tubicinem*, 1.
& invitatur
ad *Deditionem*.
Quod facere
si abnuat,
oppugnatur
ab obsidentibus
& occupatur:
Vel muros
per *Scalas* 2.
transcendendo,

or breaking them down
with Battering-engines 3
or demolishing them
with great Guns; 4.
or breaking tho-
row the Gates
with a Petarr; 5.
or casting Granadoes 6
out of Morter-pieces 7.
into the City,
by Engineers, 8.
who lye behind
League-baskets; 9.
or overthrowing it
with Mines
by Pyoneres. 10.

They that are besieged
defend themselves (from
the Walls, 11.
with Fire,
and Stones, &c.
or break out by force.
A City
that is taken by Storm,
is plundered,
destroyed,
and sometimes laid
even with the ground.

aut *Arietibus* 3.
diruendo,
aut *Tormentis* 4.
demoliendo;
vel Portas
Exostrâ 5.
dirumpendo; (6.
vel *Globos tormentarios*
è *Mortariis* (balistis) 7.
per *Balistarios*, 8.
(qui post *Gerras* 9.
latitant) in Urbem
ejaculando;
vel eam
per *Fossores* 10.
Cuniculis subvertendo.

Obsessi
defendunt se
de *muris*, 11.
ignibus,
lapidibus, &c.
aut *erumpunt*. 12.

Urbs
vi expugnata,
diripitur,
exciditur,
interdū solo æquatur.

CXLIV.

Religion. *Religio.*

Godlinefs, 1.	*Pietas*, 1.
the Queen of Vertues,	Virtutum Regina,
worfhippeth God 4.	
devoutly,	hauftâ
the knowledge of God	Notitiâ Dei,
being drawn,	vel
either from the	ex *Libro Naturæ*, 2.
Book of Nature, 2.	(nam opus
(for the Work	commendat artificem)
commendeth	vel
the work-Mafter,)	ex *Libro Scripturæ*, 3.
or from the	*colit Deum* 4.
Book of Scripture, 3.	humiliter,
She meditateth upon	recolit Mandata ejus
his Commandements	comprehenfa
contained	

in

in the Decalogue ; 5.
and treading reason
under Foot,
that Barking Dog, 6.
she giveth Faith 7.
and Assent to the
Word of God,
& calleth upon him, 8.
as a helper,
in adversity.

Divine Services
are done
in the Church : 9.
in which are,
the Quire, 10.
with the Altar, 11.
the Vestry, 12.
the Pulpit, 13.
Seats, 14.
Galleries, 15.
and a Font, 16.

All men perceive
that there is a God,
but all men do not
rightly know God.

Hence are
divers Religions (ned
whereof IV. are recko-
ret (s t) e chief.

Dicalogo ; 5.

& Rationem,

Canem oblatrantem, 6.
conculcans. *Fidem* 7.
& *ad sensum* præbet
Verbo Dei,
eumque *invocat*, 8.
ut Opitulatorem,
in adversis.

Officina divina
fiunt
in *Templo* : **6.**
in quo est,
Penetrale (Adytum) 10.
cum *Altari*, 11.
Sacrarium, 12.
Suggestus 13.
Subsellia, 14.
Ambones, 15.
& *Baptisterium*. 16.

Deum esse,
sentiunt omnes homi-
sed non omnes (nes;
recté norunt Deum.

Hinc
diversæ *Religiones*
quarum primariæ **IV.**
adhuc numerantur

CXLV.

Gentilisin. *Gentilismus.*

The Gentiles feigned to themselves neer upon XI M. Deities.	*Gentiles* finxerunt sibi prope XIIM. *Numina.*
The chief of them were Jupiter, 1. President & petty-God of Heaven;	Eorum præcipua erant *Jupiter*, 1. Cœli;
Neptune, 2. of the Sea;	*Neptunus*, 2. Maris;
Pluto, 3. of Hell;	*Pluto.* 3. Inferni;
Mars, 4. of War;	*Mars*, 4. Belli;
Apollo, 5. of Arts;	*Apollo*, 5. Artium;
Mercury, 6. of theeves; Merchants; and eloquence;	*Mercurius*, 6. Furum, Mercatorum, & Eloquentiæ;
Vulcan (Mulciber) of Fire, and Smiths;	*Vulcanus* (*Mulciber*) Ignis & Fabrorum;
Æolus, of Winds:	*Æolus*, Ventorum Præsides & *Deastri*:

and

& the most obscene of
all the rest Priapus.
They had also
Womanly Deities:
such as were
Venus, 7. the Goddess
of loves & pleasures,
with her little son Cu-
Minerva (Pallas) (pid; 8
with the nine Muses,
of Arts; (weddings;
Juno, of Riches, and
Vesta, of Chastity;
Ceres, of Corn;
Diana, of Hunting,
and Fortune;
and besides these
Morbona,
and Febris her self.
The Egyptians,
instead of God
worshipped all sorts of
Beasts and Plants,
& whatsoever they saw
first in the Morning.
The Philistines offered
to Moloch, 9.
their Children
to be burnt alive.
The Indians 10.
even at this day wor-
ship the Devil. 11.

& obscænissimus
Priapus.
Habuerunt etiam,
Muliebria Numina:
qualia fuerunt
Venus, 7. *Dea* (tatum,
amorum & Volup-
cum filiolo *Cupidine*, 8.
Minerva (*Pallas*)
cum novem *Musis*,
Artium; (ptiarum;
Juno, Divitiarum & Nu-
Vesta, Castitatis;
Ceres, Frumentorum;
Diana Venationum,
& *Fortuna*;
quin & *Morbona*,
ac *Febris* ipsa.
Ægyptii,
pro Deo colebant
omne genus (rum,
Animalium & Planta-
& quicquid manè (tur.
primùm conspicaban-
Philistæi offerebant
Molocho (*Saturno*) 9.
Infantes
vivos cremandos.
Indi 10.
etiamnum venerantur
Cacodæmona. 11.

CXLVI.

Judaism. *Judaismus.*

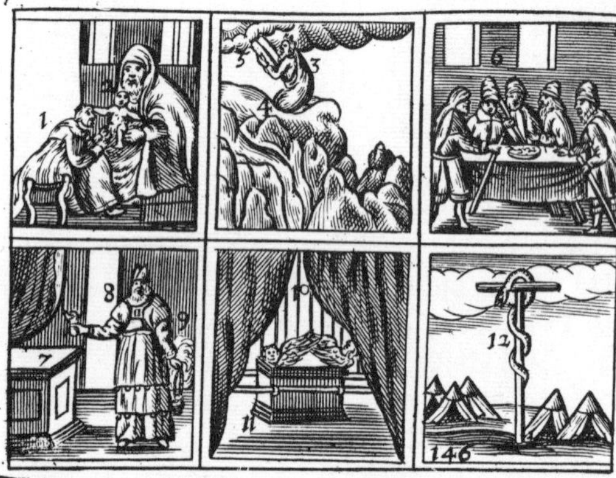

Yet the true Worship
of the true God,
remained with the
Patriarchs, who lived
before, & after the Flood.
Amongst these,
that seed of the woman
the Messias of the world
was promised to Abraham. 1. the Founder
of the Jewes,
the Father of them
that believe: and he
(being called away
from the Gentiles)
with his Posterity,

Verus tamen *Cultus*
veri *Dei*, remansit
apud *Patriarchas*,
qui vixerunt
ante & post Diluvium.
Inter hos,
Abrahamo, 1.
Judæorum Conditori,
Patri Credentium,
Promissus est,
Semen illud Mulieris,
Mundi *Messias*:
& ipse,
avocatus à Gentilibus,
cum Posteris,

being

being marked with the
Sacrament of Circum-
cision, 2. made a peculi-
ar People, and Church
Afterwards (of God.
God gave his Law
written with his own
finger
in Tables of stone; 5.
to this people
by Moses, 3.
in Mount Sinai. 4.

Furthermore he or-
dained the eating of the
Paschal Lamb : 6.
and Sacrifices to be
offered upon an Altar 7.
by Priests, 8.
and Incense : 9.
and Commanded
a Tabernacle 10. with
the Ark of the Covnant 11
to be made : & besides,
a brazen Serpent 12.
to be set up against the
biting of Serpents
in the wilderness.

All which things
were Types of the
Messias to come,
whom the Jewes
yet look for.

Sacramento Circumcisi-
notatus (*onis* 2.
singularem populum
& *Ecclesiam* Dei con-
Huic populo (stituit.
postea DEUS,
per *Mosen*, 3.
in monte *Sinai*, 4.
Legem suam,
scriptam digito suo
in *Tabulis lapideis*, 5.
exhibuit.

Porrò ordinavit
manducationē *Agni Pa-*
& *Sacrificia* (*schalis*: 6.
in *Altari* 7.
offerenda
per *Sacerdotes*, 8.
& *Suffitûs* : 9.
& jussit fieri
Tabernaculum 10.
cum *Arcâ Fœderis* : 11
prætereà erigi
æneum Serpentem 12.
contra morsum
Serpentum in deserto.

Quæ omnia
Typi erant
venturi *Messiæ*,
quem *Judæi*
adhuc exspectant.

CXLVII.

Chriſtianity. *Chriſtianiſmus.*

The only-begotten
eternal Son of God, 3.
being promiſed
to our firſt Parents
in Paradiſe, at the laſt
being conceived by
the Holy-Ghoſt,
in the moſt Holy womb
of the Virgin Mary 1
of the Royal Houſe
of David, and clad
with human fleſh,
came into the world at
Bethlehem of Judæa,
in the extreme poverty
of a Stable, 2.

Unigenitus æternus
Dei Filius, 3.
promiſſus *Protoplaſtis*
in *Paradiſo*, tandem,
impleto tempore, con-
ceptus per *Sa. Spiritum*
in utero ſanctiſſimo
Mariæ 1. *Virginis*
de domo regiâ
Davidis,
& indutus
humanâ carne,
Bethlehemi Judææ,
in ſumma paupertate
Stabuli, 2. in

in the fulness of time,
in the year of the world
3970. but pure from all
sin, & the name of Jesus,
was given him,
which signifieth
a Saviour,
when he was sprinkled
with holy Baptism, 4.
(the Sacrament of the
New Covenant) by
John his fore-runner, 5
in Jordan, the most sa-
Mystery of the (cred
divine Trinity apear'd
by the Fathers voice 6.
(whereby he testifieth
that this was his Son)
& the Holy Ghost in the
shape of a Dove, 7.
coming down from
heaven.

From that time being
the 30. year of his age,
unto the fourth year, he
declared who he was,
his words and works
manifesting his Divi-
nity, being neither
owned, nor entertain-
ed by the Jewes.

Anno mundi 3970.
in mundum prodiit,
sed mundus
ab omni *peccato*,
eiq; impositum fuit
nomen *Jesu*, (*torem.*
quod significat *Salva-*
Hic, cum imbueretur
sacro *Baptismo*, 4.
(*Sacramento*
Novi Fœderis)
à *Johanne* præcursore
in *Jordane*, (suo 5.
apparuit sacratissimum
Mysterium
divinæ *Trinitatis*,
Patris voce 6.
(quâ testabatur,
hunc esse *Filium* suum)
& *Spiritu Sancto*
in Specie *Columbæ*, 7.
cœlitus delabente.

Ab eo tempore,
XXX. ætatis suæ anno
Verbis
& Operibus,
præ se ferentibus
Divinitatem,
declaravit quis esset,
in annumusq; quartum:
à *Judæis*.

because of his
voluntary poverty.

He was at last taken
by these (when he had
first instituted
the Mystical Supper 8.
of his body and Blood,
for a Seal of
the new Covenant,
and the remembrance
of himself) carried to
the Judgement-Seat of
Pilate Governour
of Cæsarea, accused,
and condemned, as
an innocent Lamb;
and being fastened
upon a Cross; 9.
he dyed being sacrificed upon that Altar
for the sins of the
world.

But when he had
revived by his divine
power, he rose again
the third day out of
the Grave, 10.
and forty dayes after,
being taken up from
Mount Olivet, 11.
into Heaven 12.

nec agnitus nec exceptus ob voluntariā paupertatem

Ab his (quum prius instituisset
Cœnam mysticam 8.
Corporis & *Sanguinis* sui,
in Sigillum
novi Fœderis.
& sui recordationem)
captus tandem,
ad *Tribunal Pilati*
Præfecti *Cæsarei*
raptus, accusatus,
& damnatus est,
Agnus
innocentissimus;
actusq; in *Crucem*, 9.
in arâ istâ,
pro peccatis *mundi*
immolatus,
mortem subiit.

Sed tertiâ die,
quum revixisset
divinâ suâ virtute,
resurrexit
è *Sepulcro*, 10.
& post dies XL,
de *Monte Oliveti* 1.
sublatus in *Cœlum.* 12.

and

and returning thither	& eò rediens
whence he came,	unde venerat,
he vanished as it were,	quasi evanuit,
whilst the Apostles	aspectantibus
gazed upon him, 13.	*Apostolis*, 13.
to whom he sent	quibus decimâ die
his Holy Spirit 14.	post *Adscensum* suum,
from Heaven,	*Spiritum Sanctum* 14.
the tenth day	de *Cœlo*,
after his Ascension,	ipsos verò,
and them being filled	hâc Virtute
with this power,	impletos,
into the world,	de se præjudicaturos
to preach of him;	in Mundum,
being henceforth	misit;
to come again	olim rediturus
to the last Judgement,	ad *judicium extremum*,
sitting in the mean	intereà sedens
time at the right hand of the Father,	ad *dextram Patris*,
and interceding	& intercedens
for us.	pro nobis.
From this Christ	Ab hoc *Christo*
we are called	dicimur
Christians	*Christiani*,
and are saved in him (alone.	inq; eo solo salvamur.

CXLVIII.

Mahometism. *Mahometismus.*

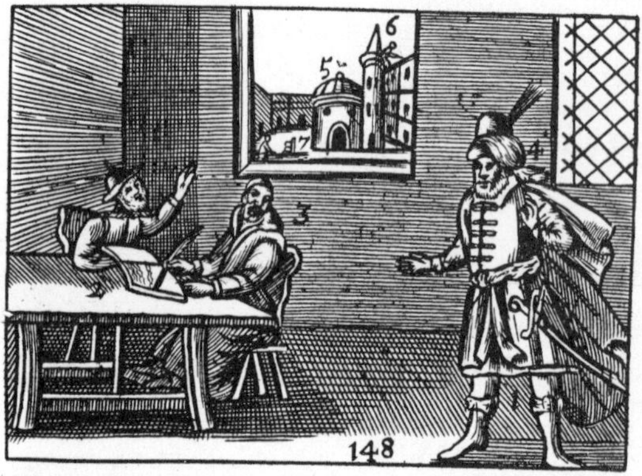

Mahomet 1.
a warlike Man,
invented to himself
a new Religion,
mixed
of Judaism,
Christianity,
and Gentilism,
by the advice of
a Jew 2.
and an Arian Monk, 3.
named Sergius;
feigning,

Mahomed 1.
homo bellator,
excogitabat sibi
novam Religionm,
mixtam
ex *Judaismo*,
Christianismo,
& *Gentilismo*,
consilio
Judæi 2.
& *Monachi Ariani*, 3.
nomine *Sergii*;
fingens,

whilst

whilst he had the fit of	dumlaboraret *Epilepsiâ*
the falling sickness, that	secum colloqui, (*lem*,
the Archangel Gabriel	*Archangelum Gabrie-*
and the Holy Ghost	& *Spiritum Sanctum*,
talked with him, using	adsuefaciens
a pigeon, 4	*Columbam*, 4.
to fetch meat	ut ex aure suâ
out of his ear.	escam peteret.
His Followers	*Asseclæ* ejus
refrain themselves	abstinent se
from Wine;	à *Vino*;
are circumcised;	circumciduntur:
have many wives;	sunt *Polygami*:
build Chappels, 5.	exstruunt *Sacella*, 5.
from the Steeples	de quorum *Turriculis*,
whereof they are called	
to holy Service,	non à *Campanis*
not by Bells,	sed à *Sacerdote* 6.
but by a Priest: 6	ad sacra
they wash themselves	convocantur:
often; 7.	sæpius se *abluunt*; 7.
they deny	negant
the Holy Trinity	*S S. Trinitatem*:
they honour Christ	*Christum honorant*,
not as the Son of God,	non ut *Dei Filium*,
but as a great	sed ut magnum
Prophet,	*Prophetam*,
yet lesse than	minorem tamen
Mahomet;	*Mahomete*:
they call their Law	*Legem* suam
the Alcoran.	vocant *Alcoran*.

God's

CXLIX.

Gods Providence. *Providentia Dei.*

Mens States,
are not to be attributed
to Fortune,
or Chance,
or the Influence of the
Stars (Comets 1.
indeed are wont to
portend no good)
but to the provident
Eye of God 2.
and to his
Governing Hand: 3

Humanæ Sortes,
non tribuendæ sunt
Fortunæ;
aut *Casui,*
aut *Siderum Influxui,*
(*Cometæ* 1. quidem
solent nihil boni
portendere)
sed provido
Dei Oculo 2.
& ejusdem
Manui rectrici, 3.

even

even our sights,
or oversights,
or even our Faults.
God,
hath his Ministers
and Angels, 4.
who accompany
a Man 5.
from his Birth,
as Guardians,
against wicked Spirits
or the Devil, 6.
who every minute
layeth wait for him,
to tempt
and vex him.
Woe be to the mad
wizzards and witches,
who give themselves
to the Devil (being
enclosed in a Circle, 7
calling upon him
with Charms)
they dally with him,
and fall from God!
for they shall receive
their reward with him.

etiam nostræ *Prudentiæ*
vel *Imprudentiæ*,
vel etiam *Noxa*.
Deus
habet *Ministros* suos
& *Angelos*, 4.
qui *Homini*, 5.
à nativitate ejus,
se associant,
ut *Custodes*, contra
Malignos Spiritûs,
seu *Diabolum*, 6.
qui minutatim
ei insidias struit,
ad tentandum
vel vexandum.
Væ dementibus
Magis & *Lamiis*
qui Cacodæmoni
se dedunt,
(inclusi *Circulo*, 7.
eum advocantes
incantamentis)
cum eo colludunt,
& à Deo deficiunt!
nam cum illo
mercedem accipient.

CL.

Judicium Extremum.

The laſt Judgement.

For the last Day
shall come,
which shall raise
up the Dead, 2.
with the sound of
a Trumpet 1.
and summon the quick
with them to the
Judgement-seat
of Christ Jesus, 3.
(appearing
in the Clouds)
to give an account
of all things done.
When the Godly
and Elect 4.
shall enter into life
eternal into the place
of Bliss and the new
Hierusalem ; 5.
But the wicked
and the damned 6.
shall be thrust
into Hell 8.
with the Devils 7.
to be there tormented
for ever.

Nam adveniet
Dies novissima,
quæ
Voce *Tuba* 1.
Mortuos 2.
resuscitabit,
& cum illis
Vivos citabit
ad *Tribunal*
Iesu Christi, 3.
(apparentis
in Nubibus) (nem
ad reddendam ratio-
omnium actorum.
Ubi *pii* (*justi*)
& *Electi* 4.
in Vitam æternam,
in locum *Beatitudinis*
& *novam Hierosolymam*
introibunt. (5
Impii vero
& *Damnati* 6.
cum *Cacodæmonibus* 7.
in *Gehennam* 8.
detrudentur,
ibi æternùm
cruciandi.

Clausula.

The Close.

Thus

Thus thou hast seen	Ita vidiſti
in ſhort	ſummatim
all things	Res omnes,
that can be ſhewed,	quæ oſtendi poterunt,
and haſt learned	& didiciſti
the chief words	*Voces primarias*
of the Engliſh & Latine	*Anglicæ* & *Latinæ*
Tongue.	*Linguæ.*
Go on now	Perge nunc,
and read other	& lege diligenter
good Books diligently,	alios bonos *Libros*,
and thou ſhalt become	ut fias *Doctus*,
learned, wiſe, & godly.	*Sapiens*, & *Pius*.
Remember theſe	Memento horum ;
things ; fear God,	Deum time,
and call upon him,	& invoca eum,
that he may beſtow upon thee	ut largiatur tibi
the Spirit of wiſdom.	*Spiritum Sapientiæ.*
Farewell.	Vale.

A.

Coqui.

Mer-

Præſtigiæ.

Terra.

INDEX TITULORUM.

An INDEX of the TITLES.

An INDEX of the TITLES.

An INDEX of the TITLES.

Trinuni Deo Gloria.